Dancing through
the dissonance

Manchester University Press

Dancing through the dissonance

Creative movement and peacebuilding

Lesley Pruitt and Erica Rose Jeffrey

Manchester University Press

Copyright © Lesley Pruitt and Erica Rose Jeffrey 2020

The right of Lesley Pruitt and Erica Rose Jeffrey to be identified as the author of this work has been asserted by them in accordance with the Copyright, Designs and Patents Act 1988.

Published by Manchester University Press
Oxford Road, Manchester M13 9PL
www.manchesteruniversitypress.co.uk

British Library Cataloguing-in-Publication Data
A catalogue record for this book is available from the British Library

ISBN 978 1 5261 4339 6 hardback
ISBN 978 1 5261 9560 9 paperback

First published 2020
Paperback published 2026

The publisher has no responsibility for the persistence or accuracy of URLs for any external or third-party internet websites referred to in this book, and does not guarantee that any content on such websites is, or will remain, accurate or appropriate.

EU authorised representative for GPSR:
Easy Access System Europe – Mustamäe tee 50, 10621 Tallinn, Estonia
gpsr.requests@easproject.com

Typeset by Toppan Best-set Premedia Limited

Contents

Preface	*page* vi
Acknowledgements	x
Introduction	1
1 Finding our rhythm: why and how to think about dance and peace	19
2 Young people as peer leaders for peace: emerging strategies	44
3 Local/global dance 'hubs' for peace	75
4 Finding empathy and practising peace through dance: through a mirror darkly?	111
5 Embodying peace: prospects for self-care within settings of conflict	141
Conclusion	164
References	174
Index	189

Preface

More and more it seems to me … that when I write, what I am really trying to do is dance, and because it is impossible, because dancing is free of language, I am never satisfied with writing … to dance is to make oneself available (for pleasure, for an explosion, for stillness) … The abstract connections it provokes in its audience, of emotion with form, and the excitement from one's world of feelings and imagination – all of this derives from its vanishing … But writing, whose goal is to achieve a timeless meaning, has to tell itself a lie about time; in essence, it has to believe in some form of immutability.
Nicole Krauss, Forest Dark (2017)

Because dance is nuanced, diverse and complex, we would like to acknowledge that the format of this book – which relies on the written word – limits our ability to fully document or understand the various ways dance can inform or facilitate peacebuilding. After all, writing about dance poses inherent challenges because it offers only one way among many of understanding and analysing dance.

We recognise that writing about dance is challenging because 'the very act of dancing always seems to evade attempts to set it down on paper'.[1] Yet we persevere in our intention to expand the dialogue around peacebuilding.

While recognising the challenges, we continue to find meaning in attempting to write about dance, or perhaps – in rare moments of inspiration – to dance writing. We hope you will follow along with us and maybe even shift perspectives and directions as we try

Preface

to work out the steps, improvise and ultimately convey meaning through the admittedly limited medium of words.

Lesley

In researching my first book, *Youth Peacebuilding: Music, Gender, and Change*, I explored the use of music as a tool to engage youth in reducing and preventing violence.[2] More specifically, the research for that book included participant observation and semi-structured interviews with young people involved in musical peacebuilding programmes in Australia and Northern Ireland. Studying these programmes provided a uniquely deep look at young people's experiences of everyday violence and how they approached peacebuilding in their local cultural contexts. That project contributed to theoretical and practical debates and discussions around youth political participation, the gendered landscape of conflict environments and creative approaches to pursuing peace. In particular, I explored how music could foster peacebuilding by offering an alternative means for dialogue,[3] helping people create and recreate identities for themselves and others,[4] and offering a tool that could help create safe spaces for such dialogue and identity work, often in challenging circumstances.

While my research has taken me in many directions in the decade since I completed the fieldwork that underpinned that first book, I always feel drawn to return to reflections on creative approaches to peace, especially the ways they can engage youth. At the best of times, this has taken the form of working to further analyse and share the findings from my research on dance and peacebuilding. While my earlier work dealt with dance as part of a broader range of musical practices for peacebuilding,[5] since then I have explored dance more specifically, and this book is the culmination of that work to date. As a lifelong lover of dance, it is a joy to be able to consider the subject in a book-length format. Moreover, having the chance to do that work in collaboration with Erica Rose, a

Preface

professional dance practitioner, offers a wonderful opportunity to challenge my own thoughts, hone my insights and, hopefully, share them with our audience in an accessible way. I thank you in advance for your patience with any missteps.

Erica Rose

As a self-proclaimed dance activist, I have an ongoing curiosity about the ways in which dance functions in our lives and societies balanced with the enquiry and reflection of academic research. Throughout my professional dance career, I have had the opportunity to glimpse many facets and varied elements of dance practice and performance. Combined with my ongoing interest and work in peacebuilding, my curiosity extends to the ways in which dance and peacebuilding interact. I also see my work as a cultural translator, between the cognitive and the embodied, striving to find the ways in which written language can convey movement. Through my doctoral research, I investigated the ways in which creative dance interacts with peacebuilding in the Asia-Pacific region, focusing on the Philippines and Fiji, working directly with local peacebuilders. My research also engaged in ongoing reflective practice regarding my role as an artist practitioner. It provided the platform to interrogate the places where my own boundaries overlap or bump into each other. My work in peacebuilding now takes me to Bougainville, Papua New Guinea, where dance continues to play a role in the interactions of local and regional peacebuilding.

    I initially connected with Lesley through research during my master's degree, and immediately felt the joy of meeting a kindred spirit interested in arts and peacebuilding, as well as having great respect for her ongoing body of work. It is a privilege to work with her and to continue to expand and deepen my own thinking around the complexities of peacebuilding and its interaction with dance. In many ways, with dance, the ideas expressed in a series of movements or gestures hold a more complex meaning than is easily

Preface

translatable to the written word. The physicality and multidimensionality of dance represent strengths, yet they also render the page an incomplete representation. I seek to continue to develop the ways in which I translate between forms, disciplines and practices, creating access without losing the essence of movement. Writing this book with Lesley continually pushed me to think beyond my established frames of reference.

Through this effort to distil the elements of dance at work in peacebuilding, rather than a dissection, I strive to gain and share a deepening understanding of dance and peacebuilding and, ultimately, to contribute to the fine-tuning or perhaps disruption of practice and ongoing inclusion of diverse worldviews in peacebuilding. This book is both a gathering and sharing of knowledge as well as an invitation to join the dance. Like any new dance, there are chances of bumping into others, yet it is from within these places of connection or possible missteps where the choreography is refined or new directions emerge. It is my hope that through this book, you will encounter new ideas and perspectives, and I thank you in advance for moving through them with us.

Shall we dance?

Notes

1 D. P. McCormack, 'Geographies for moving bodies: thinking, dancing, spaces', *Geography Compass*, 2 (2008), p. 1825.
2 L. J. Pruitt, *Youth Peacebuilding: Music, Gender, and Change* (Albany: State University of New York (SUNY) Press, 2013).
3 L. J. Pruitt, 'Creating a musical dialogue for peace', *International Journal of Peace Studies*, 16 (2011), pp. 81–103.
4 L. J. Pruitt, 'Music, youth and peacebuilding in Northern Ireland', *Global Change, Peace and Security*, 23 (2011), pp. 207–22.
5 L. J. Pruitt, 'They drop beats, not bombs: a brief discussion of issues surrounding the potential of music and dance in youth peace-building', *Australian Journal of Peace Studies*, 3 (2008), pp. 10–28.

Acknowledgements

Lesley's University of Melbourne McKenzie Postdoctoral Research Fellowship (2012–2014) provided necessary research funding for this project. RMIT University and Monash University supported Lesley during some of the writing and revisions of the manuscript. The University of Queensland and the Rotary Foundation supported Erica Rose during the fieldwork she conducted for this project, and Queensland University of Technology supported her during the writing process.

This book includes some excerpts from and revised versions of sections of the following article: L. J. Pruitt, 'Gendering the study of children and youth in peacebuilding', *Peacebuilding*, 3 (2015), pp. 157–70. Lesley is thankful to the editors of that journal, the editors of the special issue in which the article appeared and the anonymous reviewers of the article for their constructive feedback, which strengthened the writing on this project.

We are so grateful to the many generous friends and colleagues who have offered guidance, advice and support throughout this research project. Particular thanks go to: Chris Agius, Tim Aistrope, Marshall Beier, Helen Berents, Roland Bleiker, Birgit Bräuchler, Volker Boege, Mark Chou, Constance Duncombe, David Duriesmith, Sara Houston, Katrina Lee-Koo, Serge Loode, Ross Marlay, Siobhan McEvoy-Levy, Sara Meger, Florence Nulens, Avery Dorothy Howard Poole, Ceridwen Spark and Leslie Wirpsa.

Acknowledgements

We are also thankful to all of the Manchester University Press team and the anonymous reviewers who have offered constructive suggestions and feedback that have helped significantly improve our work. We hope we have adequately addressed all of their thoughtful ideas, and any errors that may remain are our own.

In sum, we would like to thank the pioneering scholars and practitioners who have stretched their imaginations and their bodies before us. We are grateful to our long-serving mentors and colleagues for their wisdom and insight. Thank you to our families and partners who stand by us in our scholarship and practice. We would also like to acknowledge our children and the inspiration they provide to create a more peaceful and dance-filled world. Finally, we are very grateful to all of the research participants and the young people around the world who are working to dance through the dissonance and embody peace.

Introduction

As a musician who works for peace, 'unity' holds less interest for me than 'harmony.' Unity is when we all sing the same note. Harmony is when we sing different notes, and they are beautiful together.

David Lamotte, musician and peace activist

This quote from David Lamotte points to important aesthetic and creative considerations. It also highlights some key related political concerns. Lamotte explains: 'Harmony is not homogeneity', and insists that, 'Creating that confluence takes attention, patience, and work … [a]nd it is not achieved by eliminating difference, but instead by finding ways to work together that are mutually nourishing, that honour and reveal each other's gifts'.[1] In this book we demonstrate how dance can encourage these elements and thus support peacebuilding.

This book explores the relationship between dance and peacebuilding in pluralist societies. It highlights instructive insights that dance can provide when reflecting on existing theories and debates around peace and conflict. Our research deepens the understanding of the roles the arts, and dance in particular, play in peacebuilding. It builds on existing work in International Relations (IR), Peace and Conflict Studies, and Dance, as well as complementary areas of study, such as anthropology, neuroscience and law. This book considers the work of a non-governmental organisation (NGO) and its participants deploying dance for youth peacebuilding through case studies in Colombia, the Philippines and the United States. This dance programme took place in several locations and in different contexts of violence or conflict and varied approaches to peace. Investigating the application of a dance-based peacebuilding programme across these three case studies allows us to consider nuance and context, as well as commonalities across the locales.

A young person designed this particular programme and most of the facilitators and participants were young people. Learning from their experiences contributes to the development of multifaceted understandings of youth in peace and conflict. The research focused on the experiences of young people, and it facilitates insights into existing debates and practical questions in relation to local–global interactions, while highlighting the possibilities for, and challenges to, dance and peacebuilding.

Our research connects with a number of practical efforts and applications. Indeed, people seeking to build peace in a variety of contexts have increasingly recognised the value of dance for peacebuilding.[2] Internationally, dance has grown in popularity as a means of connecting people and communities experiencing violence and conflict, with fellow peacebuilders around the world. Moreover, these connections have been amplified through the increased visibility and enhanced global awareness of a connection between dance and peacebuilding. Consider, for example, the global One Billion Rising (OBR) campaign, initiated by Eve Ensler.[3] Participants around the world learn the OBR choreography through online platforms, and then stage local performances in public spaces as part of a campaign to end violence against women and girls. As a global movement featuring local performances that aim to reduce and prevent violence, OBR highlights prospects for dance and peacebuilding as well as questions of agency, power relations and politics more broadly, including ideas around what constitutes 'local' and 'global' in this context.

Yet standard approaches from the United Nations (UN) or other formal organisations engaged in peacebuilding tend to render dance

Introduction

– along with other everyday politics and everyday life practices – invisible, thereby dismissing arts and dance-based approaches as 'soft' or not 'serious'.[4] Limited research has been conducted on how dance might (or might not) be implemented for peacebuilding across a range of contexts of conflict, including through conflict prevention and peace education initiatives, for example.[5] Existing scholarship considering creative approaches to peacebuilding serves as an important starting point for the work done here, but to date few studies have provided empirical analyses of what the programmes or efforts they mention do.[6]

We see the sidelining of dance as linked to IR's lack of imagination when it comes to theorising bodies and their global political significance. There is a frequent division in IR between mind and body that slights the political significance of bodies themselves. In contrast, following Wilcox,[7] we see bodies as constructed politically, socially and culturally, and thus both produced and productive. Bodies are targets of violence, but they are malleable, so they can also resist and produce different political possibilities and identities, and in the process generate new social configurations.

While most work in IR on embodiment has focused on its role in understanding violence,[8] our work deeply interrogates embodiment in relation to peace. Our book explores how reflecting on embodiment might offer new insights into peacebuilding and how dance can inform our understandings of the everyday *practice* of peace. It explores how peacebuilding through dance profoundly builds relationships across stark differences, navigates local and global aspects of peacebuilding through a terrain of common ground, and addresses challenges in everyday conflict resolution and peacebuilding practice.

This book suggests that dance, as an aesthetic, embodied medium, can support peacebuilding in its capacity to embrace emotions, support relationships across difference, supplement and sustain verbal linguistic forms of dialogue, and bridge understandings of the local and global. Through the process of exploring *how* this takes place, we illuminate prospects and challenges in the practice and study of peacebuilding and conflict transformation.

Research puzzle

As conflicts become more localised, culturally specific and complex, the need for curious, creative and critical approaches to peacebuilding and politics has grown significantly. How can the subjective have value and be connected to multiple, diverse perspectives that are essential to peacebuilding? Further exploration is essential, particularly with young people, since they are increasingly affected by conflict and war, but remain starkly marginalised from peace and reconciliation initiatives. Moreover, their lives and experiences of conflict and peacebuilding offer important insights into changing local and global contexts.

Around the world, practitioners regularly engage in innovative and reflective arts-based peacebuilding work, yet there is limited analysis available to policy makers, practitioners, scholars and the public, despite the growth in popularity of arts-based approaches to conflict transformation and reconciliation. This book offers a unique insight into the application, practice and analysis of a dance-focused peacebuilding programme and interrogates the ways in which this programme fits into global peacebuilding and local and global politics. Our book explores the experiences and perspectives of young people who engage in dance for peacebuilding in Colombia, the Philippines and the United States, and tells an important story through interrogating the interface of dance and peacebuilding.

This book builds on research in the interdisciplinary field of Peace and Conflict Studies, as well as innovations in critical IR scholarship, including research on aesthetics and global politics,[9] scholarship considering emotions and politics,[10] and feminist work that has made embodiment of the subject central to the work of

Introduction

deconstruction and emancipation.[11] Our research brings together applied activities and ongoing political analysis, including reflecting on existing theories around the politics of peacebuilding. We seek to carve out a new research agenda that can account for the politics of considering dance as an aesthetic, emotional and embodied approach to peacebuilding.

Keeping this in mind, it is important to examine the relationship between dance and peace, including prospects for emancipatory outcomes, but also the risks and challenges of arts-based approaches to peacebuilding. There are many potentially problematic, though sometimes unintended, negative consequences in attempting to quantify the effects and results of peace programmes. The creative elements of arts-based peacebuilding efforts make them more difficult to fit into standard frameworks of effectiveness measurement. Yet it is important to critically reflect continually on the efficacy of these initiatives to identify and share best practices to explore what can and cannot be measured, and to shape further empirical and analytical indicators that stem from arts practice.

In peacebuilding efforts, the dominant approach has tended to focus on technical, quantifiable solutions; yet this kind of approach can obscure the processes and frameworks necessary to pursue constructive social change. Likewise, in contrast, our framework follows the work of Lederach,[12] as we agree that an approach that can enable peacebuilders to see themselves as artists rather than as technicians supports an everyday ontology defying the reductionist tendencies of a focus on metrics and outcomes. It instead asks questions of *how* peace can be articulated and enacted through creative approaches that include actual physical movement as part of a transformative social movement for peace.

Key terms

It is worthwhile explaining the key terms used in this book, including 'dance' and 'peacebuilding', which are central concepts in our research. We offer our working definitions here, and recognise that the process of this research also continues to challenge and deepen our understanding of them.

Dance can elude definition in universalising terms because of 'its longevity and multiplicity of forms and functions'.[13] While we acknowledge that this merits ongoing reflection, we follow the definition of dance provided by Hanna, who explains dance as 'human behavior composed of purposeful, intentionally rhythmical, and culturally patterned sequences of nonverbal body movements and stillness in time and space and with effort. The movements are mostly not those performed in ordinary motor activities but may refer to them.'[14] She recognises that 'dance serves a wide spectrum of purposes, often several simultaneously'.[15] Similarly, Coe and Strachan suggest that dance is multifaceted, 'a multisensory experience that includes the visual, the spiritual, the kinesthetic, and the auditory'.[16] Moreover, following established dance educators,[17] we see dance as movement within space, time, shape and motion. We recognise that everyday movement is a basis for dance while acknowledging creative dance and movement approaches emphasising imagination, embodied problem solving and development of individual aesthetic expression.[18]

Dance is thus necessarily socially and culturally situated. Grau suggests that being able to move together in a rhythm is what has enabled individuals to work together to acquire language and, consequently, culture.[19] Likewise, for Grau, the power of dance is understood to reside in its capacity to bring together intellect, emotion and feeling.

Dance is also deeply interconnected with music. There are strong interrelations between dance and music activities in practice, participation and performance. Likewise, rather than comparing or contrasting the benefits of dance and music in peacebuilding, here we seek to increase understanding of dance in peacebuilding while continuing to refine the broader dialogue around arts and peacebuilding.

Introduction

In this book we consider dance to include a wide variety of activities that may also include professional dance performances. However, the focus of our empirical study remains on community dance activities most often centred on young people's participation in peacebuilding.

As for peacebuilding, our understanding of this concept incorporates a broad range of projects, initiatives, actions and policies that seek to prevent, reduce or assist recovery from violence and conflict in various forms. Peacebuilding thus encompasses a spectrum of actions that can include high-level UN-sponsored post-conflict peace negotiations as well as bottom-up approaches from individuals and grassroots community organisers.[20] However, our perspective focuses on a positive approach to peace, which requires 'working in a bottom-up rather than a top-down fashion … to ultimately change general cultural norms about dealing with violence'.[21] Moreover, we see this spectrum of peacebuilding as including peacebuilders' own quality of life, which is critical to the sustainability of their work,[22] though it has yet to be well explored in existing literature.

Data collection and analysis

To consider the concepts, themes and queries articulated above, this book reports on a study examining the use of dance in peacebuilding programmes across a range of contexts, including Colombia, now commonly deemed a post-conflict site;[23] the United States, specifically in inner-city locations in New York City, Washington DC and Baltimore, where violence is commonly seen as widespread;[24] and in the Philippines, which, even in the context of a signed peace agreement and steps towards the creation of an autonomous region, continues to experience conflict in the southern island of Mindanao.[25]

The programmes in all three countries were run by the same global NGO, which originated in Colombia and expanded to the

United States, the Philippines and elsewhere.[26] The NGO, which began in 2010 and is referred to here as 'Movement4Peace' (M4P),[27] ran programmes in schools and community centres to teach young people about empathy and nonviolent means for dealing with conflict. Driven by her own local and international dance experiences, a young woman developed the programme based on her belief that dance could be useful in promoting empathy and building peace. A programme was created using embodied, creative approaches to support young people in peacebuilding. M4P thus developed a series of partnerships with community-based organisations, universities, development agencies and government ministries in Colombia and the Philippines, and with schools and community groups in the US.

Implemented over a series of workshops, the programme was facilitated by a group of young peer leaders whose work incorporated dance and creative movement to involve other young people in peacebuilding. In general, each workshop began with a warm-up, then moved to a task-based dance activity, including discussion of a peacebuilding skill (e.g. expressing emotions), and then closed following a relaxation exercise. Through these physical, creative activities, dialogue and relaxation, M4P peer leaders sought to engage participants in identifying and expressing emotions, discovering and valuing difference, promoting empathy, supporting leadership development and working collaboratively to build peace.

During the time of our study, the M4P programme utilised a combination of creative movement activities, such as engaging participants in creating, sharing and copying each other's movements, or learning choreography from other global branches of the programme. While deploying a general curriculum for peacebuilding through dance and creative movement, M4P worked under the assumption that this curriculum could be adapted based on the context of the conflict and the status of peace initiatives.

By studying the programme's deployment across diverse sites, we interrogate similarities and differences, including ways

Introduction

dance may or may not work in peacebuilding efforts around the world or within a particular locale. Throughout the book, our analysis includes background and contextual information on the kinds of conflicts that are endemic to these societies as well as information on broader approaches to peace used in the various contexts.

Using participant observation, interviews and document analysis, the research presented here incorporates data collected by the authors in each of the three countries featured in the study. This intensive data gathering included Lesley participating in the NGO's full global peer leader training held in the US, as well as months of participant observation of the programmes in the US and Colombia. Meanwhile, Erica Rose similarly spent months conducting participant observation in the Philippines. This methodological approach offered rich insights into how dance and creative movement can and do engage young people in peacebuilding across a range of diverse contexts.

Semi-structured interviews cited throughout the book were conducted with peer leaders in the various locations.[28] Lesley conducted the US interviews and some Colombian interviews, while Mariana Zuluaga Mejia, a research assistant with translation capacity, completed the rest in Colombia. The ten US interviewees were all female and in their twenties. Most were from white, middle-class backgrounds, except for one young white woman from a working-class background and two young women who each had one non-white parent. Two were first-generation Americans. At the time of the interviews, all were living in Washington DC, Baltimore or New York City, working for M4P. In Colombia, ten individuals were interviewed – seven females and three males between the ages of 21 and 32. All were from middle-class families and had university qualifications. Erica Rose conducted the interviews in the Philippines as a research assistant. The ten interviews conducted there (seven females and three males) included young people aged 18–33.[29] All Filipino interviewees were high-school educated and in the process of pursuing or had completed university. Exploring the experiences of young people involved in peacebuilding in these diverse communities shows us the varied ways violence is experienced and peace is understood and enacted. The analysis also includes intersecting factors such as age and gender, which may be represented and negotiated differently in a variety of settings. The aim is not to make comparisons between the sites; rather, the inclusion of different areas helps to strengthen the data's richness.

Key themes

This book offers insights into the application and practice of a dance-based, localised peacebuilding programme, and interrogates the ways in which this programme fits into the broader global context. Incorporating the multiple elements of dance practice, participant voices and critical political analysis, this book reveals important implications and nuances regarding an arts-based peace initiative that, when applied, can offer needed understandings within the peacebuilding field. This book makes an important contribution to multiple fields and enhances understandings of the potential, challenges and political dynamics of integrating dance into peacebuilding. By exploring the politics of dancing peace, interpersonal interactions, the ability to 'practise peace', and local and global connections, this book highlights and analyses key themes in arts-based peacebuilding work. Noting the need to revise or replace existing dominant approaches to addressing conflict, the global community continues to seek ways to build peace across differences – such as race, religion, gender, culture, age and locality. Heeding these efforts, this book provides a critical in-depth analysis and recommendations for practice by exploring the benefits and challenges of arts-based peacebuilding.

In light of existing research and analysis of the data collected in this project, what can we say about dance and peacebuilding at

Introduction

this point? Firstly, participant statements indicated that 'dance can be useful in engaging youth in peacebuilding but that it must be applied in sensitive, reflexive and culturally relevant ways to appeal to, and include, both young men and young women'.[30] The inclusion of age here is salient, given the importance and growth in attention to the roles of youth in peace and conflict. This book specifically asks how, if at all, dance functioned as a useful way for youth to take part in peacebuilding. The book also goes beyond applications with youth to consider what we can learn about peacebuilding and how we can enact it through dance and creative movement across a lifetime. Key findings from the project include the ways in which dance is perceived as being useful in peacebuilding, the value of embodiment and practising peace with others, and the potential for dance to bridge perceived local–global divides.

Of the young interviewees for this project, most, if not all, participants articulated examples of how dance had been useful for peacebuilding. For example, some noted that dance served as a nonviolent means of communication and a mechanism to connect with one's feelings in a peaceful way. Dance was seen as culturally relevant and familiar, so many youth could relate to it. They also noted that dance does not always require a great deal of training or expensive equipment. Plus, participants saw dance as a way to reduce and release stress, an important part of recovering from witnessing or experiencing violence.

Participants also recognised a variety of limitations regarding what dance could do and how. For example, they identified how short-term funding cycles – often common to global peacebuilding initiatives, particularly those run by NGOs – can at times create programmes that are short-sighted. Participants pointed out that, without careful attention to inclusion and access, attempts at engaging youth in peacebuilding through dance and creative movement might overlook some people's needs – for example, people living with disabilities or those who speak a language other than the one in which programmes are delivered, such as young indigenous people in Colombia. Still, these limitations are not inherent to dance, nor are they always present, as seen, for example, in the work of VisAbility in Sri Lanka, a country recovering from conflict, where dance programming has been used to engage people with and without disabilities in coordination with a rights empowerment initiative.[31]

It appears that dance and creative movement, when applied in thoughtful ways, can help foster peacebuilding. However, dance can also be ineffective; sometimes it can even create exclusions. After all, research has uncovered connections between choreography and war,[32] including conceptualisations of how conflict is choreographed through activities such as military drills and rituals.

However, when used in thoughtful, reflexive ways in the pursuit of peace, dance can have much to offer. In one of our interviews for this research, one facilitator of programmes using dance and creative movement for peacebuilding in Washington DC and Baltimore spoke about stepping out of one's comfort zone to engage within a group:

> When one person takes a positive risk, it shows the rest of us that we can take a positive risk and encourages us to do that also. So hopefully, after a while they will be able to see that if they can just do one thing that makes them uncomfortable or kind of step outside their comfort zone that it actually helps other people to do the same and get the most out of the experience.

Such steps – both metaphorical and embodied – can surely be a useful means for reflecting on ways of finding harmony within the dissonance of conflict.

Structure of the book

While research around creative approaches to peacebuilding has inspired growing interest, several aspects remain ripe for exploration, with dance remaining particularly under-studied. We are pleased

Introduction

to have this opportunity to continue the scholarly conversation while exploring new dimensions and pointing to new directions for the future. Each chapter of this book seeks to depict the complex and multidimensional interactions between dance and peacebuilding. The chapters are structured as follows.

Chapter 1 considers dance in relation to peacebuilding; it interrogates existing research from across a range of fields of study, including law and development studies and the key disciplines informing this research project: Peace and Conflict Studies, IR, and Dance. The chapter explores how growing interest and research in arts-based peacebuilding highlight the importance of utilising multiple pathways in the pursuit of peace. It also examines how dance and music are recognised globally as important facilitators of social cohesion and the creation and expression of culture. The chapter considers theories and practices of dance and peacebuilding, including discussions of embodiment and empathy, among other key concepts. This exploration provides context to understand how and where dance and peacebuilding meet. We argue for recognising the important roles dance can play in encouraging diverse forms of communication, building relationships across difference and engaging the participation of diverse actors in local, national and international forums.

Chapter 2 discusses the role of young people in peacebuilding and the ways in which dance plays a part in this process. Previous research has identified the importance and political significance of young people in peacebuilding.[33] International organisations such as the UN have also made steps to increase the opportunities and support for young people in peacebuilding endeavours, locally and globally, for example through the passage of UN Security Council resolutions 2250 and 2419 on Youth, Peace and Security in 2015 and 2018, respectively. Despite these efforts, and the extent to which youth are immersed in conflict both as recipients of violence and as perpetrators, young people remain on the sidelines of peace initiatives and are not sufficiently recognised and engaged in policy, theory or practice. This research suggests that dance can constitute an effective, inclusive pathway to support youth participation in peacebuilding. At the same time, the data gathered highlights the importance of including options for peace, reconciliation and social transformation that are age appropriate, gender sensitive, culturally relevant and flexible.

Chapter 3 considers the creation and sharing of 'hub dances' – group dance exchange activities – across and between programme sites, to investigate what dance can tell us about local and/or global approaches to peacebuilding, including how these two different types of approaches are defined, interact, or may co-constitute one another. It also examines the political ramifications of this co-creation and/or interchange. The hub dances are envisioned to serve as a vehicle for cross-cultural moments of exchange and to provide opportunities for (re)creating identities in ways that can support peacebuilding. The use of hub dances also prompts further examination of the different cultural contexts in which conflict occurs. The practice also prompts reflection on the tensions between dance styles featuring individual or group freedoms versus the homogenisation of dance ideas. In short, complexities around hub dances help us to think through the possibilities of instilling stereotypes and/or being valued for difference. We consider the ways in which the creation, practice and exchange of hub dances enacts meaning around the identities of self, others and the community, and how this relates to the creation of broader social change for peacebuilding.

Chapter 4 explores practising peace by investigating a set of activities involving the use of mirroring movements. Cultivating empathy has been identified as one crucial element of building peace. As researchers have established, empathy is essential to the restructuring of relationships after violence. Mirroring is a well-established dance activity that is used in many settings and contexts, including theatre, dance therapy, dance education and community dance. Simple variations are also included in some mainstream

Introduction

peacebuilding resources as icebreakers. The case studies across cultures demonstrate that peace must be practised, and the process of mirroring provides opportunities for this. It invites interpersonal exchange and builds kinaesthetic, or felt, empathy, which provides avenues through which to see, understand and feel others across difference. In addition to the potential of empathy within peacebuilding, this chapter discusses the politics of empathy and its challenges in arts-based peacebuilding.

To date, practitioner self-care is underexplored in Peace and Conflict Studies, even though peacebuilders themselves could benefit immensely from further investigation in this area, which could in turn strengthen the depth and quality of their work as facilitators for peace. The research for this book suggested that participants had an opportunity to experience themselves in ways that enabled them to express a deeper sense of self-understanding, embodiment and strength to go on with their work. Beginning with an exploration of the practice of relaxation embedded in the programme and across the case studies, in Chapter 5 we consider how, in the midst of difficult work in conflict-ridden circumstances, peacebuilders have embraced the opportunities that dance provides to relieve stress and re-engage with their bodies. Chapter 5 acknowledges that diverse bodies may be placed differently in settings of conflict. It also interrogates the prospects and challenges posed by gender and age norms in particular sites of peacebuilding. We suggest that dance has broader implications in peacebuilding because it can help enable a more reflective stance for considering conflict. In this sense, it has the potential to offer new, creative directions for pursuing peace.

The conclusion summarises the key points of the preceding chapters and identifies implications for theory and practice. It considers how creative approaches such as dance have specific applications in relation to peacebuilding and why they matter more broadly. It also discusses the wider use of arts in peacebuilding and proposes suggestions for future relevant research.

Notes

1 D. Lamotte, *World Changing 101: Challenging the Myth of Powerlessness* (Black Mountain: Dryad Publishing, 2014), p. 113.
2 E. Beausoleil, 'Dance and neuroscience: implications for conflict transformation', in *The Choreography of Resolution*, ed. by M. LeBaron, C. MacLeod and A. F. Acland (Chicago: American Bar Association, Section of Dispute Resolution, 2013), pp. 55–80; M. Eddy, 'Dancing solutions to conflict: field-tested somatic dance for peace', *Journal of Dance Education*, 16 (2016), pp. 99–111; E. R. Jeffrey and L. J. Pruitt, 'Dancing it out: building positive peace', in *Dance and the Quality of Life*, ed. by K. Bond (New York: Springer, 2018), pp. 475–93.
3 For more detailed discussion of OBR, see D. Mills, 'Dancing the ruptured body: One Billion Rising, dance and gendered violence', in *Dance and Politics: Moving Beyond Boundaries* (Manchester: Manchester University Press, 2017), pp. 83–98.
4 M. Shank and L. Schirch, 'Strategic arts-based peacebuilding', *Peace and Change*, 33 (2008), pp. 217–42.
5 Jeffrey and Pruitt, 'Dancing it out'; L. J. Pruitt, *Youth Peacebuilding: Music, Gender, and Change* (Albany: State University of New York (SUNY) Press, 2013); Shank and Schirch, 'Strategic arts-based peacebuilding'.
6 For example, J. P. Lederach, *The Moral Imagination: The Art and Soul of Building Peace* (Oxford: Oxford University Press, 2005); L. Schirch, *Ritual and Symbol in Peacebuilding* (Bloomfield: Kumarian Press, 2005).
7 L. B. Wilcox, *Bodies of Violence: Theorizing Embodied Subjects in International Relations* (Oxford: Oxford University Press, 2015).
8 For a notable exception, see H. Berents, 'An embodied everyday peace in the midst of violence', *Peacebuilding*, 3 (2015), pp. 1–14; H. Berents, *Young People and Everyday Peace: Exclusion, Insecurity and Peacebuilding in Colombia* (New York and London: Routledge, 2018).
9 R. Bleiker, *Aesthetics and World Politics* (New York: Palgrave Macmillan, 2009).
10 E. Hutchison, *Affective Communities in World Politics: Collective Emotions after Trauma* (Cambridge: Cambridge University Press, 2016).
11 Wilcox, *Bodies of Violence*.
12 Lederach, *The Moral Imagination*.
13 K. Bond, 'Dance and quality of life', in *Encyclopedia of Quality of Life and Well-being Research*, ed. by A. C. Michalos (Dordrecht: Springer, 2014), p. 1419.
14 J. L. Hanna, 'A nonverbal language for imagining and learning: dance education in K-12 curriculum', *Educational Research*, 37 (2008), pp. 492.
15 J. L. Hanna, *To Dance is Human* (Chicago: University of Chicago Press, 1979), p. 35.

Introduction

16 D. Coe and J. Strachan, 'Writing dance: tensions in researching movement or aesthetic experiences', *International Journal of Qualitative Studies in Education*, 15 (2002), p. 507.
17 D. S. Blumenfeld-Jones, 'Bodily-kinesthetic intelligence and the democratic ideal', in *Multiple Intelligences Reconsidered*, ed. by J. L. Kincheloe (New York: Peter Lang, 2004), pp. 119–31.
18 A. G. Gilbert, *Creative Dance for All Ages: A Conceptual Approach* (Reston: American Alliance for Health, Physical Education, Recreation and Dance, 1992); R. Laban, *Laban's Principles of Dance and Movement Notation* (London: Macdonald & Evans, 1975); P. Reedy, *Body, Mind & Spirit in Action* (Berkeley: Luna Dance Institute, 2015); S. Stinson, *Dance for Young Children: Finding the Magic in Movement* (Washington DC: American Alliance for Health and Physical Education, 1988).
19 A. Grau, 'Why people dance – evolution, sociality and dance', *Dance, Movement and Spiritualities*, 2 (2015), p. 241.
20 H. W. Jeong, *Peace and Conflict Studies: An Introduction* (Aldershot: Ashgate Publishing, 2000); C. Zelizer and R. A. Rubinstein, eds, *Building Peace: Practical Reflections from the Field* (Sterling: Kumarian Press, 2009).
21 L. R. Forcey and I. M. Harris, *Peacebuilding for Adolescents: Strategies for Educators and Community Leaders* (New York: Peter Lang Publishing, 1999).
22 Jeffrey and Pruitt, 'Dancing it out'.
23 J. R. A., 'Why Colombia's peace deal is taking so long to implement', *The Economist* (19 June 2017), available at: www.economist.com/blogs/economist-explains/2017/06/economist-explains-18 (accessed 18 December 2017).
24 'Crime and despair in Baltimore', *The Economist* (29 June 2017), available at: www.economist.com/news/united-states/21724399-america-gets-safer-marylands-biggest-city-does-not-crime-and-despair-baltimore (accessed 18 December 2017).
25 R. J. Heydarian, 'Mindanao crisis: a city on fire', Al Jazeera (26 May 2017), available at: www.aljazeera.com/indepth/opinion/2017/05/philippines-marital-law-rekindling-horrific-memories-170526131438289.html (accessed 18 December 2017).
26 At the time of our study, the NGO was also involved in a brief trial run of a programme in Germany but the organisation's leaders advised us this initiative was unlikely to be carried forward, so given limits of funding and capacity we opted to focus on the main longer-term sites of the programme in Colombia, the Philippines and the US.
27 A pseudonym has been chosen for the organisation to preserve the anonymity of research participants in sites with small numbers of interviewees.
28 All interviewees will be referred to using a pseudonym to protect their anonymity.

29 Ethics approval was obtained from the University of Melbourne Human Research Ethics Committee, 2012, Ethics ID: 1237906, 'From youth violence to youth peacebuilders'.
30 L. J. Pruitt, 'Gendering the study of children and youth in peacebuilding', *Peacebuilding*, 3 (2015), pp. 157–70.
31 For more on VisAbility, see http://visability.social/visability-in-sri-lanka/.
32 G. Morris and J. R. Giersdorf, eds, *Choreographies of 21st Century Wars* (Oxford: Oxford University Press, 2015).
33 T. A. Borer, J. Darby, and S. McEvoy-Levy, *Peacebuilding After Peace Accords: The Challenges of Violence, Truth, and Youth* (Notre Dame: University of Notre Dame Press, 2006); K. Huynh, B. d'Costa and K. Lee-Koo, *Children and Global Conflict* (Cambridge: Cambridge University Press, 2015); S. McEvoy-Levy, 'Youth as social and political agents: issues in post-settlement peace building', Kroc Institute Occasional Paper #21:OP:2 (Notre Dame: Kroc Institute's Research Initiative on the Resolution of Ethnic Conflict, 2001); A. McIntyre and T. Thusi, 'Children and youth in Sierra Leone's peacebuilding process', *African Security Review*, 12 (2003), https://doi.org/10.1080/10246029.2003.9627222; Pruitt, *Youth Peacebuilding*; S. Schwartz, *Youth and Post-Conflict Reconstruction: Agents of Change* (Washington DC: United States Institute of Peace Press, 2010).

1
Finding our rhythm: why and how to think about dance and peace

Reach out to those you fear.
Touch the heart of complexity.
Imagine beyond what is seen.
Risk vulnerability, one step at a time.
   John Paul Lederach, *The Moral Imagination* (2005)

We start our first chapter with the words that John Paul Lederach, renowned scholar of international peacebuilding, used to finish his book over a decade ago, because we believe they speak directly to the heart of how dance and peacebuilding can connect, illuminating what dance can offer to both our understandings of peace and our everyday practices of creating peace. Lederach's words hint at a dance initiated by a reach, followed by a tactile connection and the risk of taking the next unknown step. At the same time, the excerpt highlights the need to critically interrogate challenges and to be open to the ever-evolving and messy process of peace, which is just what we aim to do through our explorations of dance and peacebuilding.

In this chapter, we make the case for considering dance in relation to peacebuilding, based on an interrogation of existing research from across a range of fields of study – from neuroscience, to law, to development studies – as well as from the key disciplines informing this research project: namely Peace and Conflict Studies, IR and Dance. This chapter explores how growing interest and research in arts-based peacebuilding highlight the importance of investigating multiple pathways in the pursuit of peace and uncovering how dance and music are globally recognised as important to the creation and expression of culture and in facilitating social cohesion.

Recognising this, the chapter considers theories and practices of dance and peacebuilding alongside relevant key concepts, such as embodiment and empathy, in order to provide context for exploring dance and peacebuilding. We argue for recognising the important role of dance in encouraging diverse forms of communication, building relationships across difference and engaging the participation of diverse actors in local, national and international forums. Finally, we introduce a basic typology of six categories for understanding dance-based peacebuilding efforts: therapeutic; artist-led social change or protest; community-led social change or protest; collective forms; educational; and diplomatic.[1]

Creating peace

As Lederach suggests,[2] we believe that peace and positive social change require both skill – which has been the main focus of most peacebuilding initiatives – and art, which has remained underexplored for far too long. Further consideration of art is necessary for building positive peace, which goes beyond the mere absence of war and includes 'the rebuilding of genuine community in areas that have suffered from great divisions and violence'.[3] Because we tend to know more about how to end harmful actions than we do about how to build settings and relationships of peace, addressing the lack of constructive curiosity when it comes to peacebuilding is critical. After all, as Lederach argues: 'Transcending violence is forged by the capacity to generate, mobilize, and build the moral imagination.'[4] Furthermore, Lederach proposes that

> the moral imagination requires the capacity to imagine ourselves in a web of relationships that include our enemies; the ability to sustain a paradoxical curiosity that embraces complexity without

reliance on dualistic polarity; the fundamental belief in and pursuit of the creative act; and the acceptance of the inherent risk of stepping into the mystery of the unknown that lies beyond the far too familiar landscape of violence.[5]

We share his belief that the wellspring of peacebuilding rests in the moral imagination and his acknowledgement that such imagination is difficult and messy, but also necessary for constructive social change. Lederach envisions such constructive social change as choosing love over fear to pursue peacebuilding that 'seeks to change the flow of human interaction in social conflict from cycles of destructive relational violence towards cycles of relational dignity and respectful engagement'; this process is thus 'defined by openness and accountability, self-reflection and vulnerability'.[6] Within this paradigm, the arts are a key area of consideration in the arena of peacebuilding.

Historically, the arts have been a means of bringing people together, even across differences, and they have contributed to the promotion of peacebuilding and reconciliation.[7] For example, Shank and Schirch suggest that art can be used to create safe spaces for healing,[8] while Ayindo submits that the arts can be a tool to foster sustainability and creativity in peacebuilding.[9] Abu-Nimer similarly proposes that the arts can help foster hope and confidence in peacebuilding.[10] Art can also help highlight aspects of conflict while offering 'opportunities to *reframe* familiar situations, encourage fresh thinking and cultivate new perspectives'.[11] In particular, research suggests that arts that incorporate performance, such as music and theatre, can contribute to the transformation of conflict in a variety of settings and environments. Furthermore, the arts can reach audiences that may be inaccessible through other means.[12]

Why dance and peacebuilding?

A steadily growing body of research demonstrates ways that dance may facilitate creative connections for engaging in relationships across difference and for transforming conflict to build peace.[13] Dance has frequently been used as a metaphor within peacebuilding, politics and diplomacy to describe the multilayered, complex interactions that are frequently evoked across cultures.[14] Yet, to date, little work has been done to unpack these metaphors beyond their descriptive capacity in order to investigate more deeply the dynamic connections between dance and peacebuilding. Doing so is worthwhile in that dance can make visible and affect the intricate webs of relations that exist in settings of conflict and that must be understood to pursue peace.[15] Jeffrey extends this idea, arguing that the arts can bring people together across differences, thereby creating the spaces around which the intricate webs of relationships are woven.[16]

When discussing physical movement and feeling in relation to our broader understandings and experience of the world around conflict and peacebuilding, it makes sense to consider bodies and embodiment. Since the Age of Enlightenment in the eighteenth century, entrenched views of body–mind separation have dominated Western thought.[17] For a significant period of time, Western thought, which in turn has dominated scholarly approaches, has privileged 'rational functioning, often to the exclusion of other senses and intelligences', and such thought systems have likewise existed in a state of being '"disembodied" because they block access to, and reject, ways of being and knowing that explicitly engage the body'.[18]

Understandably, the highly embodied world of dance has received inadequate attention in terms of meaning-making, since such views have 'discounted, dismissed, and overridden the very body that dance brings to the fore'.[19] This makes it unsurprising that, despite people and organisations using dance to address conflict around the world, such practices have rarely garnered significant scholarly attention in the 'canon' of approaches to addressing conflict.[20] On the contrary, in this book, we suggest that embodied approaches have central roles to play in peacebuilding; thus, bodies cannot

Finding our rhythm

be ignored, either in studies of dance or in other approaches to transforming conflict.

After all, dance is a physical form of communication. The embodied, physical approach dance offers is an important means to deepen and diversify peacebuilding practice in tangible, visible ways. Just as we need to attend to bodies to better understand violence, we must take this enquiry further to address the pursuit of peace through embodied forms of expression. As Wilcox so eloquently states, 'it is incumbent upon us to think through ways in which we live in and through bodies, and of the complex movements and formation of such bodies, which may serve as a site for creatively rethinking our future political horizons'.[21]

An embodied perspective, which dance is uniquely placed to offer, is felt and seen, and thus presents an immediate challenge to politics and the status quo in connecting the perceived rational mind and the allegedly separate and more irrational body.[22] Discussions of the mind and body in peace are connected to questions about the role of creativity in peacebuilding. Scholars, practitioners and those affected by conflict have frequently called for enhanced creativity in the implementation of peace initiatives. However, few analyses provide insights into what this creativity actually looks like, how and where it is being practised and its effect on the body politic of processes of peacebuilding, conflict resolution and reconciliation at the community, national and global levels.

Dance has received little attention in the broader literature considering the arts and peacebuilding. It certainly deserves more consideration, given its relevance to a range of local and global concerns related to peace and conflict, and increasing international interest in the role of the arts in peacebuilding. Åhäll writes: 'Dance is an understudied topic in IR, yet at the same time it seems that dance is "everywhere" in global politics.'[23] Existing research has suggested that, while governments can use dance to exert ideological control, citizens can also use dance to resist political repression and build community in the midst of violence, as well as to challenge the State and create new political futures.[24] For example, consider the multiple ways in which dance is used to support the government agenda in Rwanda,[25] or how in Brazil the practice of capoeira has been used as a form of resistance to the neoliberal order.[26] While such research has not focused explicitly on peacebuilding and dance, it points to the importance of situating dance in relation to social justice, which is a crucial component of positive peace and thus a key goal for peacebuilding. At the same time, other important recent research by legal scholars has investigated links between dance and conflict resolution, advocating that conflict resolution training should incorporate movement practices that provide potential benefits to both affected parties and the mediation practitioners themselves.[27]

Existing dance and conflict transformation research suggests that dance is significant for peacebuilding because it can play an important role in how people understand themselves and others, including in settings of conflict. The outcomes of dance and how they are actualised can be diverse, which is unsurprising since dance can be integral to people's particular ways of life.[28] Dance can create and remake identities;[29] and, through its relationality, dance can serve as a key factor in human evolution.[30] Likewise, dance can be used to incite violence;[31] and it can serve the cause of nationalism, colonialism or conquest.[32] Yet dance can also be a way of knowing and a means of embodying cultural knowledge and creating connections,[33] including the creation of community identity,[34] and a persistent means of communication even within systems of racial segregation.[35]

Dance, as Head points out, has the potential to foster constructive communication, trust and healing, all of which are key pursuits of peace.[36] A number of scholars have documented the potential dance holds for fostering empathy.[37] Meanwhile, Siapno suggests that dance may play an important role in fostering resilience and self-care for peacebuilders themselves; moreover, she does so while advocating for a locally generated perspective based in cultural practice rather than only on external intervention.[38] Finally, Eddy argues that dance can support the creation and expression of body–mind connections by serving as an avenue for communicating both ideas and emotions.[39] Eddy further points to research finding that dance can be used to resolve incidents that could potentially lead to violence, eliminate tension and/or offer education on nonviolent conflict resolution.[40]

Given all of these prospects and reflections from our own previous work, in this book we aim to take bodies and embodiment seriously in our understanding of peacebuilding. We do so because we believe bodies matter politically in a range of ways, including in the immediate lived sense of experiencing peacebuilding and in the ways we understand pressing global political questions. Indeed, like Aistrope we affirm 'the body as a crucial presence in the meaning-making process'.[41]

Ways dance and peacebuilding meet

Reflecting on these examples and others from practice, it is possible to identify some differing, though often overlapping, methods of deploying dance in relation to peacebuilding. In surveying the field, we have proposed a basic typology of six categories that we identified and mapped to conceptualise efforts of dance-based peacebuilding:

- **Therapeutic**: The American Dance Therapy Association (www.adta.org) defines dance movement therapy (DMT) as 'the psychotherapeutic use of movement as a process which furthers the emotional, cognitive, physical, and social integration of the individual'. Several DMT practitioners work as peacebuilders around the world, including in post-conflict settings and with internally displaced people and refugees.
- **Artist-led social change or protest**: Artists lead dance performances to support peacebuilding. These artists see audiences as both witnesses and prospective change agents who use the

power of aesthetic engagement to share meaning and to explore ideas that can contribute to peacebuilding.
- **Community-led social change or protest**: These dance activities are inclusive and incorporate a transformative process for the creators and performers, and they aim to connect people across differences. Likewise, in these contexts, social change that fosters peacebuilding can occur across boundaries or within a community itself.
- **Collective forms**: In these participatory dance activities, a group seeks to enact change and focuses on community transformation or affirmation. Likewise, the purpose may be to develop group consciousness or to engage different groups in collective efforts that foster peacebuilding.
- **Educational**: Dance is used as a tool of peace education. In this sense, dance can be strategically utilised to support other forms of learning or to provide a tool for relaying important knowledge and skills for peacebuilding, including around themes of conflict resolution, principles of nonviolence, and emotional and social intelligence.
- **Diplomatic**: Dance can also be used in formal and informal diplomatic efforts, such as during the Cold War period when performance tours were one of the few modes of communication between the Soviet Union and the United States. Diplomatic dance commonly also occurs in international peacebuilding events or programmes when cultural nights or local dance performances are presented by participants, sometimes professionals, in an effort to help members of diverse audiences get to know one another and show respect for difference.[42]

We do *not* suggest that these categories are all-inclusive or that we have identified all ways that dance has been or can be used for peace. Rather, we provide this preliminary typology in an effort to promote the variety of potential applications of dance in relation to peacebuilding. We believe this process contributes to mapping the field to better understand peacebuilding more broadly. This enables us to reflect on how different approaches to dance might operate in different peacebuilding efforts or contexts. It also helps us to identify, recognise and honour a broader cohort of peacebuilders who actively engage in efforts to reduce, prevent or promote recovery from conflict.

Of course, we also recognise that there are limits to this approach. For example, when an initiative has not been studied in detail, these categorisations are necessarily based on the publicly stated intent of a programme or initiative, which may not always directly reflect the underlying beliefs or intentions of the facilitators and/or participants. Although a distinction between different dance-based approaches is possible, some efforts may defy categorisation, while others may exhibit crossover by fitting into more than one of the categories or changing over time. Hence, these categories can best be understood as fluid and intersectional, always evolving, much like the art of dance and the practice of peacebuilding. Rather than being static, they are porous, interactive and relational. Similarly, all the categories should remain open to interrogation, because all of them can be deployed in ways that may hinder rather than foster peace if they are not used critically and reflectively.

Where dance and peacebuilding meet

Dance and peacebuilding meet perhaps most visibly in the public eye in the metaphorical sense. News reports, op-eds and other public writing frequently use 'dance' along with associated terms like 'choreography', 'flexibility', 'steps' and 'partners' discursively when discussing efforts at, or prospects for, diplomacy, peace negotiations and the prevention or resolution of interstate conflicts.

Dance metaphors have been used to describe a wide range of political actors over decades, for example in the following description of the diplomatic relations of North and South Korea: 'The choreography behind this peace process is … going to be tricky.

The bonding may have begun among the leaders, and more small steps may be taken, but there are limits on how far this can go without moves that make a material difference.'[43] The following year, in an article on the political situation in Ireland titled 'Complex dance to save the peace agreement', the author reported: 'Confirmation that the Irish Republican Army has started to put arms beyond use is the latest piece of complex political choreography aimed at restoring Northern Ireland's institutions and saving the Good Friday Peace agreement.'[44]

Such depictions are not limited to parties in conflict or state leaders; they are also deployed in relation to UN officials. For example, in a 2014 *New York Times* article titled 'For U.N. chief, a dance of diplomacy is halted by a misstep', the reporter stated: 'Over the weekend, Ban Ki-moon, the United Nations secretary general, with a reputation for being risk averse, took a significant risk. He choreographed a precise diplomatic sequence on Syria that relied on others to perform their roles equally precisely. The choreography did not go as planned, and Mr. Ban stumbled under the spotlight.'[45]

Similar language has also been used to describe countries that are predicted to face conflict in the future and that need to 'dance' well to avoid it, for example in an article titled 'Asia's "cold peace": China and India's delicate diplomatic dance', which speaks of 'the potential to set early limits to efforts by Washington, Tokyo and others to engage India as a security partner in the present ballet of Asian power balancing'.[46] Further, in describing Xi Jinping's actions, the article states that, 'the implications for regional security are almost as worrying as if he had personally choreographed the border push'.[47] Using dance discursively hints at the ways in which the complexities of building peace are envisioned through the sense of movement and choreography.

At the same time, the role of dance in peacebuilding expands beyond the metaphorical sense, occurring in material, physical spaces all around the world, including in countries facing, recovering

Finding our rhythm

from or working to prevent a wide range of types of violence and conflict. For example, media reports have documented how the National Ballet of Rwanda, which includes Rwandan dancers from different sides of the conflict, many of whom were refugees or had family members killed in the unrest, performed at home and abroad in an attempt to share a message of reconciliation and to show people of all ages that 'dance can make everybody more peace-loving'.[48] Reports from Liberia similarly tend to confirm this, indicating that young people there use krumping – a highly energetic, all-body street dance – individually, with friends or in dance crews to help deal with stress or anger. The creative expression of these emotions can be an important aspect of recovery for the first generation that lived through the conflict to experience their teenage years after a war.[49] In 2017, South African researchers suggested that dance education experiences provide an embodied physical way to explore and resonate with 'South Africa's motto of "Unity in Diversity"'.[50]

Similarly, in 2001 the *Guardian* reported how a Sri Lankan performance troupe made up of former refugees and soldiers affected by conflict and who were living with disabilities, frequently told their stories of war in performances that included drama, music and dance. Touring internationally even as the war continued, these performers evidenced 'an astonishing ability to understand, forgive and focus on the future' and, in doing so, they worked to connect across difference. As one young woman explained: 'I was nervous at first ... We used to know only Tamils, but now we've got to know other communities. It's like a bridge.'[51] Then, in 2012, Sri Lankan youth from different backgrounds celebrated the International Day of Peace by incorporating dance; during the event they learned about nonviolent communication and violence prevention.[52]

There is growing awareness of how dance has been used in peace efforts as a means to connect local and global actors. For example, youth in Kigali, Rwanda, celebrated International Day of Peace in an event that featured six artists from different African countries who came together to perform a peace anthem, aimed at working towards a united Africa.[53] Additionally, during key stages of the peace process in Bougainville, Papua New Guinea, UN peace monitors performed the traditional Maori dance the haka as a way to build trust and cultural understanding.[54]

The incorporation of dance and creative movement in peacebuilding efforts is not limited to countries currently experiencing or recovering from civil wars. In some cases, peacebuilding efforts may be aimed at supporting peace through dance internationally, such as the case of a US university student who designed a project to collect donations of ballet shoes and clothes to support a dance for peace programme in Iraq that aimed to unify people of different religions and heritages in Kurdistan.[55] The US State Department actively engages dance in the context of soft diplomacy through its DanceMotion USA programme supporting American contemporary dance companies in a series of international cultural exchanges.[56] At the same time, dance performances in the US have been an important feature of concerts aimed at bringing together people from different countries and cultures to promote peace internationally,[57] and of performances in which school students aim to spread a message of peace to their peers and parents.[58]

Our own previous research has documented a number of practical examples of the use of dance for peace around the world. This has ranged from the use of krumping and break dance in an Australian community peace initiative for youth,[59] to dance during peacebuilding training programmes in the Philippines,[60] to creative movement and community peacebuilding workshops in multiple locations in Fiji.[61]

Movement4Peace

As outlined in the Introduction, the research conducted for this book examined the use of dance and creative movement in peacebuilding in Colombia, the Philippines and the US through the programmes of an international NGO. While international partners contributed locally created content, staff members working at the organisation's main leadership base in the US developed most of the general curriculum. Having already outlined details of how the programmes looked and functioned, here we briefly provide background for the local and national contexts in which these programmes operated. This is a useful step to take before we move into how the programme worked for peace, because it offers a deeper understanding of how activities and concepts are created, recreated and translated in different contexts and what the prospects and limits to such local/global peacebuilding practices may be.

The NGO responsible for the programmes analysed in this book originated in Colombia, and later expanded to the US and the Philippines. In the following sections, we provide a brief introduction to the contextual backgrounds of peacebuilding for each of these case study sites. Understanding that each of these sites have deeply complex histories of conflict, peace and trauma, this introduction to the case study sites merely provides a starting place for discussion.

Colombia

Several armed groups took part in the Colombian conflict, including left-wing guerrilla groups such as the Revolutionary Armed Forces of Colombia (FARC), the National Liberation Army (ELN), government forces, crime syndicates and right-wing paramilitary groups. After several setbacks, Colombia's peace accord was ratified in late 2016, thus officially ending the conflict, which was the longest armed conflict in the history of the Americas, lasting well over half a century. While these groups had different reasons for their participation, in general the conflict is typically understood to have begun with the era known as *La Violencia*, which began following presidential candidate Jorge Eliécer Gaitánin's assassination in 1948. The conflict unleashed intra-party violence that claimed approximately two hundred thousand lives. At the same time, it is important not to oversimplify the causes of the Colombian conflict, as they were diverse and many.[62] Over the many years the conflict went on, Colombians were deeply affected, with several significant waves of internal displacement.[63] Estimates in 2012 suggested 3.9–5.3 million people had been displaced during the conflict.[64]

In the face of this challenging and complex context, a number of Colombians went to great efforts to advance the cause of peace.[65] In response to the worst violence, which occurred in the 1990s, the Colombian peace movement grew in strength with diverse actors working to address political, social and economic problems that were causing, or escalating, the violence.[66] Nonetheless, peace groups were often left out of formal peace dialogues, which were held largely between the government and leftist guerrilla leaders, despite scholars arguing that 'the most innovative and energetic peace and conflict-resolution efforts are currently most visible at the local – not the national – level'.[67]

In this context, a young American woman developed M4P in Bogotá while she was living there. M4P must be understood from within a framework based on certain culturally specific key concepts. As explained by the then country director in a staff document, in Colombia these include – among other concepts and issues – trauma, violence, peace education and movement. Trauma is understood as a common consequence of certain events featuring different types of shocking occurrences of violence, which may include direct violence, physical or psychological violence, and violence experienced or witnessed when undergone by family members, including those who may have died or disappeared during the conflict. The staffer explained that violence had become so normalised that people's hearts had become 'very tough', but noted that, at the same time, a dynamic and diverse movement of people had been working to create a myriad of alternatives to violence.

Peace education was identified as an important concept and practice for schools, social organisations and community groups.

Finding our rhythm

Often seen as related to creativity, peace education in Colombia has been aimed at preventing violence, building social conscience, protecting one another, and creating a sense of community. It has also been directed towards assisting young people to overcome vast indifference resulting from years of conflict, prompting them to learn how to express their feelings and thoughts.

To this end, movement was seen conceptually and pragmatically as highly relevant since, as the facilitator explained in an unpublished internal document: 'Movement is something that is in the DNA of Colombian culture. Movement is related to dance, and dance is part of all the cultures in Colombia' (cultures here refers to AfroColombian, indigenous, Raizal and Rom communities). Overall, she said, in Colombia, music and dance are learned, but they are also 'part of the essence of Colombian culture', and the way they are practised can differ in different regions. At the same time, heterogeneity is clearly evident in whether and how Colombians dance. According to the facilitator: 'Colombian people are recognised as awesome dancers, but there are some people that do not really like dancing because they enjoy the music without movement.'

The Philippines

Like Colombia, the Philippines has experienced a significant history of violent conflict. Comprising over 7,600 islands, the Philippines is home to a population of over ninety-five million people. Despite the signing of a peace agreement framework in 2014 and movement towards the creation of an autonomous region, the country continues to face conflict, particularly in Mindanao, the southernmost island of the Philippines where M4P leaders were based at the time of the research. People in Mindanao speak a variety of languages and subscribe to diverse religious groups, for example Christians (settlers or migrants), Lumads (non-Muslim indigenous peoples) and Moros (Muslims).[68]

In Mindanao the long-running conflicts have been caused, and/or inflamed, by different goals, perceptions and histories under a context of colonisation, including the Moro or Muslim (fourteenth century), Spanish (1565) and American (1898) periods. Martial law under the authoritarian regime of President Marcos, starting in 1972, was also a brutal period;[69] many Filipinos suffered tremendously until the People Power Revolution in 1986–1987 ended Marcos's rule. [70]

Conflict in Mindanao involving the Moro National Liberation Front and the Moro Islamic Liberation Front has persisted for over forty years. The signing of the Bangsamoro Framework Agreement in March 2014 brought hope for a possible end to the conflict, but even with the possibility of peace, longstanding cultural prejudices persist. Such prejudices are frequently cited as a reason for the conflict in Mindanao, with a Muslim minority existing alongside a Christian majority. Over three centuries of colonial rule helped to cultivate these prejudices. The Spanish colonial administrators propagated negative identities of the Moro group in Mindanao based on their own interactions with Muslims in North Africa.[71] The US colonial government continued to support negative images of Muslims while befriending other groups in the Philippines, contributing to the conflict by labelling and classifying the people, imposing discriminatory provisions on public land laws and implementing resettlement programmes.[72]

As in Colombia, M4P was delivered in the Philippines within a framework based on certain culturally specific key concepts, again including trauma, violence, bullying, peace education and movement. Within the diverse setting of Mindanao, the facilitator explained that children who are in a minority group based on ethnicity, sociocultural or economic factors often experience bullying based on cultural stereotypes when they join a class of the dominant population, and this often leads to trauma for those children. In fact, he himself reported having experienced this earlier in his life. Those not directly engaged in violent conflict, he noted, tend to experience direct violence only when people around them are inebriated; many have experienced trauma in the home environment, which can lead them to act out against others. For school children, this may be expressed through bullying, often affecting young people with disabilities.

In this wider setting, peace education became important, particularly since the former Filipino president passed an executive order supporting the teaching of peace education at all age levels. However, community efforts supporting peace education had already been well developed in the Mindanao context. As the facilitator explained, in this context, dance and movement can serve as relevant aspects of peace education and peacebuilding, since 'dance is part of the Filipino culture'. As he further explained in an unpublished internal document:

> Prior to the advent of European colonizers in the ... 1500s, the Filipinos [were] governed with ... distinct sociocultural practices and festivities. Such festivities are always associated with dance and creative movement. They usually imitate the movements of what is present in nature, such as that of the birds, wild animals, and waves of the sea. With the coming of the colonizers, the Spaniards introduced different kinds of movements. Until now, these Spanish-anchored movements are present in religious festivities in almost all of the 7,600 islands of the country. Muslims in the south, who were never colonized, have a distinct perspective on movement.

Collective dance has a strong presence in Filipino society as a component of acceptance and inclusion.[73] It is clear that, as in the Colombian case, dance and creative movement have important cultural resonance in the Philippines, but this is also clearly varied and at times contested in diverse settings.

The United States

While not having experienced a traditional civil or interstate war on domestic soil for a very long time, the United States continues to rival other countries of its economic status in levels of violence and conflict, and the gun-related murder rate is exponentially higher than in other developed nations. This is manifested in part in a history of deadly school shootings, horrific events that are much more common in the US than elsewhere.

M4P worked in the US in inner-city locations where violence in the community is widespread, including Washington DC, Baltimore and New York City. As in the other sites, M4P implemented programmes in these US cities within a framework based on certain culturally specific key concepts, again including trauma, violence, bullying, peace education and movement.

Across these contexts, a range of types of violence and bullying were present. For example, facilitators noted that in New York City, the students they worked with regularly experienced or witnessed violence, including gang violence, random violent crimes and domestic violence. Based on this experience and the lack of positive and supportive role models, many of the students became engaged in violence themselves. Likewise, the facilitators noted, Washington DC faces a great deal of gang violence, while in Baltimore drug-related violence is common. People live in racially segregated neighbourhoods in various contexts. Problems with bullying existed as well, with emotional bullying and cyber bullying most prevalent in New York City and physical bullying most prevalent in the DC and Baltimore areas.

Given these violence-affected settings, facilitators noted that the young people they worked with had often experienced trauma due to emotional or sexual abuse, gang violence or other physical violence, as well as in losing family members to violence. While noting that their aim was not to provide trauma therapy, the facilitators emphasised the importance of being sensitive to the needs of students affected by various types of violence-related trauma.

Within this context, M4P's approach to peace education in New York City focused on anti-bullying, empathy and tolerance. Because the city is so diverse, a key aim was helping students to become aware and accepting of their differences. Meanwhile, based as they are in what are known to be two of the nation's most dangerous cities, with violent crime rates exponentially higher than many locales, the DC and Baltimore area programmes focused on violence prevention and community building. M4P initiatives strove to use dance and creative movement to help educate students to express anger and deal with stress and social pressure in nonviolent ways while creating community in a safe space. This is especially important in the face of the dominance of gang violence, since recruitment to such gangs is facilitated when youth lack other ways of being part of a community. With this in mind, dance and creative movement were deployed in various ways, using an age-specific curriculum and localised choices of music and dance styles.

Facilitators in the US suggested in an unpublished internal document that 'depending on the cultural background of a person, movement can either be an integral part of their lives or a forbidden pleasure', and noted that the organisation had not always been able to find a way to transcend such boundaries. While noting that some students have at times had to contend with attempted or actual parental restrictions on their participation in movement-based activities, facilitators nonetheless emphasised that for many students 'movement is considered an integral part of' their lives. Therefore: 'Teachers try to integrate movement and the arts into curriculums, and schools are trying to provide more creative programmes.'

Next steps

This chapter focused on the theoretical framework for dance and peace, describing the contexts in which the research occurred. The next chapter examines the *who* question of this research. Specifically, because the programmes we have studied were created, designed and delivered almost entirely by young people, this study is directly situated as a contribution to understanding youth involvement in peacebuilding.

Notes

1. E. R. Jeffrey and L. J. Pruitt, 'Dancing it out: building positive peace', in *Dance and the Quality of Life,* ed. by K. Bond (New York: Springer, 2018); T. Acarón, 'The practitioner's body of knowledge: dance/movement in training programmes that address violence, conflict and peace' (PhD thesis, University of Aberdeen, 2015); C. Cohen, 'Arts and building peace: affirming the basics and envisioning the future', *Insights*, Summer (2015).
2. J. P. Lederach, *The Moral Imagination: The Art and Soul of Building Peace* (Oxford: Oxford University Press, 2005).
3. *Ibid.*, p. 41.
4. *Ibid.*, p. 5.
5. *Ibid.*
6. *Ibid.*, p. 42.
7. C. Cohen, R. G. Varea and P. O. Walker, eds, *Acting Together I: Performance and the Creative Transformation of Conflict* (New York: New Village Press, 2011); N. Premaratna and R. Bleiker, 'Art and peacebuilding: how theatre transforms conflict in Sri Lanka', in *Palgrave Advances in Peacebuilding: Critical Developments and Approaches*, ed. by O. P. Richmond (Basingstoke: Palgrave Macmillan, 2010), pp. 376–91; O. Ramsbotham, 'Conflict resolution in art and popular culture', in *Contemporary Conflict Resolution*, ed. by O. Ramsbotham, H. Miall and T. Woodhouse (Cambridge: Polity, 2011), pp. 347–58; C. Zelizer, 'The role of artistic processes in peace-building in Bosnia-Herzegovina', *Peace and Conflict Studies*, 10 (2003), pp. 62–75.
8. M. Shank and L. Schirch, 'Strategic arts-based peacebuilding', *Peace and Change*, 33 (2008), pp. 217–42.
9. B. Ayindo, 'Arts approaches to peace: playing our way to transcendence?', in *Peacebuilding in Traumatized Societies*, ed. by B. Hart (Boulder: University Press of America, 2008), pp. 185–204.
10. M. Abu-Nimer, 'Toward the theory and practice of positive approaches to peacebuilding', in *Positive Approaches to Peacebuilding: A Resource for Innovators*, ed. by C. Sampson *et al.* (Washington DC: PACT Publications, 2003), pp. 13–23.
11. Jeffrey and Pruitt, 'Dancing it out', original emphasis.
12. Cohen, Varea and Walker, *Acting Together I.*
13. M. Eddy, 'Dancing solutions to conflict: field-tested somatic dance for peace', *Journal of Dance Education*, 16 (2016), pp. 99–111; L. Koshland, J. Wilson and B. Wittaker, 'PEACE through dance/movement: evaluating a violence prevention program', *American Journal of Dance Therapy*, 26 (2004), pp. 69–90; M. LeBaron, C. MacLeod and A. F. Acland, eds, *Choreography of Resolution: Conflict, Movement, and Neuroscience* (Chicago: American Bar Association, Section of Dispute Resolution, 2013).

Finding our rhythm

14 L. Åhäll, 'The dance of militarisation: a feminist security studies take on "the political"', *Critical Studies on Security*, 4 (2016), pp. 154–68; T. Ney and E. Humber, 'Dance as metaphor: the metaphor of dance and peace building', in *The Choreography of Resolution*, ed. by M. LeBaron, C. MacLeod and A. F. Acland (Chicago: American Bar Association, Section of Dispute Resolution, 2013), pp. 81–108.
15 Lederach, *The Moral Imagination*.
16 E. R. Jeffrey, 'Dance in peacebuilding: space, relationships, and embodied interactions' (PhD thesis, Queensland University of Technology, 2017).
17 N. Alexander and M. LeBaron, 'Dancing to the rhythm of the role-play, applying dance intelligence to conflict resolution', *Hamline Journal of Public Law and Policy*, 33 (2012), p. 333; A. Grau, 'Dancing bodies, spaces/places and the senses: a cross-cultural investigation', *Journal of Dance and Somatic Practices*, 3 (2011), pp. 5–24.
18 Alexander and LeBaron, 'Dancing to the rhythm of the role-play'.
19 E. Beausoleil, 'Dance and neuroscience: implications for conflict transformation', in *The Choreography of Resolution*, ed. by M. LeBaron, C. MacLeod and A. F. Acland (Chicago: American Bar Association, Section of Dispute Resolution, 2013), p. 79.
20 E. Beausoleil and M. LeBaron, 'What moves us: dance and neuroscience implications for conflict approaches', *Conflict Resolution Quarterly*, 31 (2013), p. 134.
21 L. B. Wilcox, *Bodies of Violence: Theorizing Embodied Subjects in International Relations* (Oxford: Oxford University Press, 2015).
22 Eddy, 'Dancing solutions to conflict'.
23 Åhäll, 'The dance of militarisation', p. 162.
24 N. Jackson and T. Shapiro-Phim, eds, *Dance, Human Rights, and Social Justice: Dignity in Motion* (Lanham: Scarecrow Press (now Rowman & Littlefield), 2008); D. Mills, *Dance and Politics: Moving Beyond Boundaries* (Manchester: Manchester University Press, 2017), p. 18.
25 C. Plancke, 'Dance performances in post-genocide Rwanda: remaking identity, reconnecting present and past', *Journal of Eastern African Studies*, 11 (2017), pp. 329-46.
26 Z. Marriage, 'Evading biopolitical control: capoeira as total resistance', *Global Security*, 32 (2018), p. 275.
27 LeBaron, MacLeod and Acland, *Choreography of Resolution*.
28 K. Foreman, 'Dancing on the endangered list: aesthetics and politics of indigenous dance in the Philippines', in *Moving History/Dancing Cultures: A Dance History Reader*, ed. by A. Dils and A. Cooper Albright (Middletown: Wesleyan University Press, 2001), pp. 384–9.
29 N. Rowe, 'Dance and political credibility: the appropriation of Dabkeh by Zionism, Pan-Arabism, and Palestinian nationalism', *Middle East Journal*, 65 (2011), pp. 363–80.

30 A. Grau, 'Why people dance – evolution, sociality and dance', *Dance, Movement and Spiritualities*, 2 (2015), pp. 233–54.
31 J. Gonye, 'Mobilizing dance/traumatizing dance: Kongonya and the politics of Zimbabwe', *Dance Research Journal*, 45 (2013), pp. 64–79; J. L. Hanna, 'Dance and the "Women's War"', *Dance Research Journal*, 14 (1981), pp. 25–8.
32 Rowe, 'Dance and political credibility'.
33 M. Marx and A. Delport, '"I am because we are" dancing for social change!', *Educational Research for Social Change*, 6 (2017), pp. 56–71; D. Sklar, 'Five premises for a culturally sensitive approach to dance', in *Moving History/Dancing Cultures: A Dance History Reader*, ed. by A. Dils and A. Cooper Albright (Middletown: Wesleyan University Press, 2001), pp. 30–2.
34 L. Schirch, *Ritual and Symbol in Peacebuilding* (Bloomfield: Kumarian Press, 2005).
35 Marx and Delport, '"I am because we are"'; Mills, *Dance and Politics*, p. 15.
36 N. Head, 'Tango: the intimate dance of conflict transformation', Open-Democracy (22 August 2013), available at: www.opendemocracy.net/en/transformation/tango-intimate-dance-of-conflict-transformation/ (accessed 14 October 2019).
37 Beausoleil and LeBaron, 'What moves us'; A. Behrends, S. Müller, and I. Dziobek, 'Moving in and out of synchrony: a concept for a new intervention fostering empathy through interactional movement and dance', *The Arts in Psychotherapy*, 39 (2012), pp. 107–16; C. Berrol, 'Neuroscience meets dance/movement therapy: mirror neurons, the therapeutic process and empathy', *The Arts in Psychotherapy*, 33 (2006), pp. 302–15; K. Dunphy, M. Elton and A. Jordan, 'Exploring dance/movement therapy in post-conflict Timor-Leste', *American Journal of Dance Therapy*, 36 (2014), pp. 189–208; L. M. McGarry and F. A. Russo, 'Mirroring in dance/movement therapy: potential mechanisms behind empathy enhancement', *The Arts in Psychotherapy*, 38 (2011), pp. 178–84.
38 J. Siapno, 'Dance and martial arts in Timor Leste: the performance of resilience in a post-conflict environment', *Journal of Intercultural Studies*, 33 (2012), pp. 427–43.
39 Eddy, 'Dancing solutions to conflict'.
40 *Ibid.*
41 T. Aistrope, 'Popular culture, the body and world politics', *European Journal of International Relations*, 1 (2019), pp. 1–24.
42 For further details and examples on this and the other categories, refer to Jeffrey and Pruitt, 'Dancing it out'. See also Acarón, 'The practitioner's body of knowledge'; Cohen, 'Arts and building peace'.
43 L. Freedman, 'Moon Jae-in's diplomatic dance towards peace with North Korea', *New Statesman* (26 September 2018), available at: www.

newstatesman.com/world/asia/2018/09/moon-jae-s-diplomatic-dance-towards-peace-north-korea (accessed 14 October 2019).
44 J. Murray Brown, 'Complex dance to save the peace agreement', *Financial Times*, US edn (24 October 2001).
45 S. Sengupta, 'For U.N. chief, a dance of diplomacy is halted by a misstep', *New York Times* (22 January 2014), available at: www.nytimes.com/2014/01/22/world/middleeast/for-un-chief-a-dance-of-diplomacy-is-halted-by-a-misstep.html?_r=0 (accessed 4 January 2018).
46 R. Medcalf, 'Asia's "cold peace": China and India's delicate diplomatic dance', Brookings (24 September 2014), available at: www.brookings.edu/opinions/asias-cold-peace-china-and-indias-delicate-diplomatic-dance (accessed 4 January 2018).
47 *Ibid.*
48 S. H. Verhovek, 'Rwandans share peace and unity through dance', *New York Times* (26 ay 2000), available at www.nytimes.com/2000/05/26/us/purdy-journal-rwandans-share-peace-and-unity-through-dance.html (accessed 14 October 2019).
49 T. Ford, 'For Liberian youth, a creative outlet in krumping', *All Things Considered*, National Public Radio (17 September 2012), available at: www.npr.org/2012/09/17/161283651/for-liberian-youth-a-creative-outlet-in-krumping (accessed 14 October 2019).
50 Marx and Delport, '"I am because we are"', p. 68.
51 J. Steele, 'Dancing with the enemy: they should hate each other, but a group of Sri Lankans have found peace through dance', *Guardian* (3 May 2001), available at: www.theguardian.com/culture/2001/may/03/artsfeatures1 (accessed 14 October 2019).
52 US Agency for International Development, 'Sri Lankan youth celebrate International Day of Peace through song, dance and sport', ReliefWeb (26 September 2012), available at: https://reliefweb.int/report/sri-lanka/sri-lankan-youth-celebrate-international-day-peace-through-song-dance-and-sport (accessed 14 October 2019).
53 S. Arslanian, 'How music and dance can nurture peace', *New Times* [Rwanda] (25 September 2015), available at: www.newtimes.co.rw/section/read/192883 (accessed 4 January 2018). For critiques of how dance is used in Rwanda as a means of political instrumentalization, see Plancke, 'Dance performances in post-genocide Rwanda'.
54 V. Boege, P. Rinck and T. Debiel, 'Local–international relations and the recalibration of peacebuilding interventions: insights from the "laboratory" of Bougainville and beyond', INEF report (Duisburg: Institute for Development and Peace, University of Duisburg-Essen, 2017), p. 22.
55 'Western Michigan University student uses dance to promote peace in Iraq', *WMU News* (16 April 2010), available at: www.wmich.edu/wmu/news/2010/04/060.shtml (accessed 14 October 2019).

56 C. Croft, 'Dance returns to American cultural diplomacy: the U.S. State Department's dance residency program and its after effects', *Dance Research Journal*, 45 (2013), pp. 23–39; K. Wessel, 'DanceMotion USA: dance diplomacy for the 21st century', *Dance Informa* (2 February 2016), available at: www.danceinforma.com/2016/02/02/dancemotion-usa-dance-diplomacy-for-the-21st-century/ (accessed 23 February 2018).
57 G. Cowan and A. Aresenault, 'Moving from monologue to dialogue to collaboration: the three layers of public diplomacy', *Annals of the American Academy of Political and Social Science*, 616 (2008), pp. 10–30; 'A resolution recognizing the Alvin Ailey American Dance Theater for 50 years of service to the performing arts', S. Res. 490, 110th Congress (2008), available at: www.govtrack.us/congress/bills/110/sres490/text (accessed 9 ay 2017).
58 E. Miels, 'Performing for peace: youth event to showcase music, dance, poetry, art', *Leader-Telegram* (30 April 2015), available at www.leadertelegram.com/Entertainment/local-entertainment/2015/04/30/Performing-for-peace.html (accessed 4 January 2018).
59 L. J. Pruitt, 'They drop beats, not bombs: a brief discussion of issues surrounding the potential of music and dance in youth peace-building', *Australian Journal of Peace Studies*, 3 (2008), pp. 10–28; L. J. Pruitt, *Youth peacebuilding: Music, gender, and change* (Albany: State University of New York (SUNY) Press, 2013); L. J. Pruitt, '"Fixing the girls": neoliberal discourse and girls' participation in peacebuilding', *International Feminist Journal of Politics*, 15 (2013), pp. 58–76.
60 Jeffrey and Pruitt, 'Dancing it out'.
61 Jeffrey, 'Dance in peacebuilding'.
62 S. Elhawary, 'Violent paths to peace? Rethinking the conflict-development nexus in Colombia', *Colombia Internacional*, 67 (2008), pp. 84–100.
63 V. Sanford, 'Peacebuilding in a war zone: the case of Colombian Peace Communities', *International Peacekeeping*, 10 (2003), p. 117; Jeffrey and Pruitt, 'Dancing it out'.
64 Watchlist on Children and Armed Conflict, 'No one to trust: children and armed conflict in Colombia' (New York: Watchlist on Children and Armed Conflict, 2012). For more details on the conflict in the period leading up to the recent peace process, see V. M. Bouvier, ed., *Colombia: Building Peace in a Time of War* (Washington DC: United States Institute of Peace, 2009).
65 A. Isacson and J. R. Rodriguez, 'Origins, evolution, and lessons of the Colombian peace movement', in *Colombia: Building Peace in a Time of War*, ed. by V. M. Bouvier (Washington DC: United States Institute of Peace, 2009), p. 21.
66 C. Lopez Montaño and A. Garciá Durán, 'The hidden costs of peace in Colombia', in *Colombia: Essays on Conflict, Peace, and Development*, ed. by A. Solimano (Washington DC: The World Bank, 2000), pp. 78–158.

67 Isacson and Rodriguez, 'Origins, evolution, and lessons', p. 36.
68 C. J. Montiel, R. B. Rodil and J. M. de Guzman, 'The Moro struggle and the challenge to peace building in Mindanao, Southern Philippines', in *Handbook of Ethnic Conflict*, ed. by D. Landis and R. D. Albert (New York: Springer, 2012), pp. 71–89.
69 R. May, 'The Philippines: the ongoing saga of Moro separatism', in *Diminishing Conflicts in Asia and the Pacific: Why Some Subside and Others Don't*, ed. by E. Aspinall, R. Jeffrey and A. Regan (Abingdon and New York: Routledge, Taylor & Francis Group, 2013), pp. 221–34.
70 *Ibid.*; R. Cagoco-Guiam, 'Mindanao: conflicting agendas, stumbling blocks, and prospects toward sustainable peace', in *Searching for Peace in Asia Pacific: An Overview of Conflict Prevention and Peacebuilding Activities*, ed. by A. Heijams, N. Simmonds, and H. van de Veen (Boulder: Lynne Rienner, 2004), pp. 483–504.
71 Montiel, Rodil and de Guzman, 'The Moro struggle', p. 76.
72 *Ibid.*; Cagoco-Guiam, 'Mindanao'.
73 F. C. Williams, 'The embodiment of social dynamics: a phenomenon of Western pop dance within a Filipino prison', *Research in Dance Education*, 14 (2013), p. 51.

2
Young people as peer leaders for peace: emerging strategies

I think being young ... I think my generation gets a lot of heat for being the 'me generation' and focusing on ... Facebook or how involved we are with the Internet or on music or whatever. But I think that there are some really powerful people who are doing some really impressive things and I just want to be a part of that. I see that there is all this opportunity ... I think the first step is educating yourself about just what is going on and then how you can help fix it or contribute. And I think that we can do it. I think that my generation has the resources and we are pissed off enough and we are idealistic enough that we can do it and I am grateful to be surrounded by friends who have similar ideals and who do good things in their own way. And I think it's an exciting time to be a young person. I think that we are seeing another revolution and it's kind of like the peace movement in the [19]60s and [19]70s. I think that even though there might not be a draft or anything, I think we see that there is a war at home on just the people in general for a variety of reasons, whether it be poverty, you see the drug war. I feel like there is war on education ... I feel like there are so many things that we need to fight for and I think that a lot of my peers feel the same way and so a lot of them are doing socially conscious things and I want to be a part of that.

'Kaylee', M4P facilitator, Washington DC

The young woman from the United States quoted above clearly articulates how she sees age and generation as relevant to the roles people can and do play in peacebuilding. This theme emerged with a number of other interviewees across all of the case study sites. M4P was founded by a young woman and was almost entirely led by young people as peer leaders at the time this research was

Young people as peer leaders for peace

conducted. As a result, observations of and interviews with the young leaders offer important insights into the dynamics of the use of dance and peacebuilding, and into youth experiences in peace and conflict more broadly. This chapter discusses the roles of young people in peacebuilding and the ways in which dance and creative movement can play a part in this process. The research conducted for this book suggests that dance can constitute an effective, inclusive pathway to support youth participation in peacebuilding. At the same time, the data gathered across the three case studies highlights the importance of developing approaches that are age specific, gender sensitive, culturally relevant and flexible.

Youth, peace and security

At least as far back as the beginning of the UN in 1945, the idea existed that the need for peace extends beyond the current generation of adults. Indeed, the preamble of the founding charter of the UN begins by stating: 'We the Peoples of the United Nations determined to save succeeding generations from the scourge of war … [pledge] to reaffirm faith in fundamental human rights, in the dignity and worth of the human person, in the equal rights of men and women and of nations large and small'.[1] While this might arguably indicate a longstanding commitment to intergenerational leadership, or at least to intergenerational justice, historically, when it comes to peacebuilding, the UN has typically focused on formal political initiatives such as peace negotiations, elections and institution building.[2] While certainly important, these activities alone are not enough to ensure peace. Furthermore, young people often find it very difficult, if not entirely impossible, to participate in formal political decision-making for peace.[3]

Often below the age of franchise and thus barred from voting or holding political office, young people have had little to no access to formal involvement in most peace processes. This exclusion affects a significant proportion of the global population, especially people in conflict-affected areas. In fact, the UN Office of the Secretary-General's Envoy on Youth in the '#YouthStats' report on armed conflict noted that '[m]ore than 600 million youth live in fragile and conflict-affected countries and territories', and that '[o]f the 1.5 billion people living in fragile contexts around the world, 40% are youth'.[4] Even though they represent such a significant cohort, young people are often ignored when it comes to peace and security efforts, or, when they are considered, they are typically stereotyped as victims lacking agency rather than as active peacebuilders.[5] Therefore, their needs and concerns are often sidelined under the assumption that youth can and will access 'trickle-down' benefits from adult-centric, more 'general' efforts at peace.[6] Of course, young people can perpetrate violence, and they 'are clearly subject to the same delimiting ideologies and policies regarding national identity … as anyone else'.[7] For example, young people can be co-opted as active agents in conflicts as child soldiers, often encouraged or pressured by their communities to participate in violence.[8]

Nevertheless, young people around the world take on a variety of roles in settings of peace and conflict. They may act as perpetrators, peacebuilders and/or victim-survivors of violence, and they may over time inhabit various combinations of these roles. They participate in peace in a variety of ways, so it is important to look beyond the more formal and obvious modes of peacebuilding to identify those ways in which youth are more likely to be active.

While addressing the omission of young people from formal, high-level peacebuilding efforts is important, so too is supporting and recognising the ways youth *are* involved in peacebuilding, including in a range of everyday ways that incorporate dance and creative movement, and youth-led peacebuilding initiatives.[9] After all, Sylvester suggests that there is an 'everyday realm to international relations' where 'empathetic cooperation' may occur.[10] Her work, alongside that of other feminist IR scholars, has contributed to the shift toward investigating the everyday when it comes to peace and security. In this way, some leading scholars have constructively disrupted IR as a discipline, expanding its boundaries to go beyond national security (understood militarily), causes of war and interstate relations.[11]

Mainstream IR continues to remain caught up in Western-centric understandings of the world that depend on liberal-realist theories and that envision government elites and institutions as positioned far away from, and above, everyday society and life.[12] Since 2008, however, those pushing the bounds of the discipline, and thus supporting interdisciplinary work like ours, have made a case for examining various concepts of peace by looking at institutions from below and by connecting with everyday life.[13] Moreover, scholars advancing these new directions for understanding peace suggest that social movements, individuals and communities that critique a range of non-state actors and governance structures hold most of the potential in struggles for resisting violence and advancing social justice and human rights, all crucial elements for securing positive peace.[14] As interpreted here, peacebuilding necessarily includes these grassroots efforts at empowering people to bridge divisions to create positive change, to build institutions that can aid in preventing violence in various forms, and to heal and restore conflict-affected communities.[15]

On the whole, young people are significant demographically, but also in the many ways they are affected by and take part in conflict and peacebuilding. Indeed, it has become abundantly clear that young people 'are significant actors in peace and conflict',[16] and that this applies for girls and young women as well as for young men and boys.[17] Scholarly interest and evidence has continued to grow with regard to understanding and documenting young people's experiences and perspectives within diverse contexts of peace and (in)security, including their political significance in these scenarios.[18]

Since 2015, international organisations such as the UN have advanced towards increasing the opportunities and support for young people's involvement peacebuilding endeavours, locally and globally, including, for example, the passage of UN Security Council Resolutions (UNSCR) 2250 (2015) and 2419 (2018) on Youth, Peace and Security. Passed unanimously, UNSCR 2250 recognised the advocacy of many youth-led organisations in focusing on the range of roles youth are playing and can play in peacebuilding broadly speaking, and particularly in conflict-affected settings. UNSCR 2250 incorporates five pillars related to youth and peace: prevention, protection, participation, partnerships, and disengagement and reintegration. In doing so, the resolution makes important strides towards recognising diversity in the roles youth play in conflict and peace, and towards breaking down stereotypes that narrowly situate youth as solely or mostly victims or perpetrators.[19] Building on UNSCR 2250, UNSCR 2419 called all relevant actors to look for ways to increase young people's representation in peace agreements, both in their negotiation and implementation, and noted that the marginalisation of youth hinders sustainable peace and is detrimental to efforts at countering violent extremism.

It is also important to note here that defining 'youth' in any sort of universal way would be problematic and likely to marginalise important contextual distinctions and complexity. In fact, even various constituent parts of the UN and related organisations articulate different age ranges to fall within the scope of 'youth' or 'young people'. For example, while UNSCR 2250 on Youth, Peace and Security uses the age range of 18–29, the UN Habitat (Youth Fund) expands the scope to include young people and young adults from 15 to 32 years of age; meanwhile, a number of other bodies have a narrower scope, with the UN Secretariat, UN Children's Fund (UNICEF), World Health Organization, UN Population Fund (UNFPA), International Labour Organization and UN Educational, Scientific and Cultural Organization (UNESCO) all using the age range of 15–24 to represent youth.[20] The African

Young people as peer leaders for peace

Union Commission, on the other hand, has an even wider range, covering 15–35 year-olds.[21] Likewise, we recognise that the concept and experience of youth differ across the sites studied here, and aim to engage with that complexity throughout our analyses where possible.

Moving forward, deepening scholarly understandings of youth involvement in peacebuilding remains crucial. This book and the sites studied in it provide a glimpse at how young people in diverse communities experience violence and conflict as well as how they understand and enact peace. Through the use of interviews and participant observation, this research provides a space for youth voices to be considered. A key element that emerged in this research was the importance of age or generation, and the nexus between these and other intersecting characteristics in developing an understanding of whether and how people will participate in violence and/or peacebuilding. We turn to exploring this theme in the following section.

When young peacebuilders move for peace

As indicated in this chapter's opening quote, the young people interviewed for this book often saw the relevance of age or generation in terms of how young people experience or participate in violence or conflict, whether and how they do peacebuilding, and how the wider community responds to these involvements. For example, in Colombia, interviewees discussed the benefits of having young people's perspectives included in peacebuilding processes and practices, including their passion for peace, their capacity for generating social change, their enhanced creativity, their wish for a different future, their energy and vitality, and their curiosity and open-mindedness. Still, the theme of legitimacy came up as a challenge for young people's involvement, because even though young people may feel quite capable at peacebuilding, they often struggle to have their capacity and ability to participate recognised.

Dancing through the dissonance

Overall, facilitators from both Colombia and the Philippines echoed many of the sentiments outlined at the beginning of this chapter in the quotation from the peer leader who explained what being a young peacebuilder feels like for her. However, other participants also explained and contextualised their feelings and perspectives in terms of their own embedded locations:

> When you're young, maybe you're more creative, and I would say that my generation has seen all the conflict and violence, so we are very aware of what is happening and, being young gives us the capacity to create and do many activities. As a matter of fact, all the activities in which I participated lately have all been very creative and are all led by young people who are fighting for this country and who want to see a different future. ('Valeria', Colombia)

> I am 24 years old, but I believe that I have the influence of peacebuilding. I believe what our Philippine national hero Dr Jose Rizal said – the youth is the hope of the fatherland. And I believe in that. I am 24 years old, but I believe I am the hope of the fatherland. The Philippines is a group of 7,107 islands. We're seen by the world as a third-world country. It is very poor, and I live in a family that is very poor. My father didn't have work. My mother never worked. I had to struggle myself to work in a canteen, in a café, just to finish my college ... and now I am [here at this global training] ... So, I mean, youth is really powerful. And I believe that peacebuilding, my efforts, through [M4P] in the Philippines would be a means to help our problems there ... sometimes though the [older people] don't believe in our capacity. So, I mean, [they say things to young people like] 'who are you, by the way?' or, 'how old are you?' ... But I believe that it [the work young peacebuilders are doing] will really mean a lot. It's just a matter of believing in yourself. ('John', Philippines)

As the second statement indicates – with its gendered allusions to the home country as a 'fatherland' and its situating of the experience of economic hardship as framing his work as a peacebuilder – adequate understanding of young people's roles in conflict and in peacebuilding requires considering a range of intersecting factors.

Young people as peer leaders for peace

These include gender, ethnicity and class, all which affect young people's lives. The next section covers a range of these factors and, noting that all are clearly important to our understanding, it introduces and develops an intersectional framework to guide this research. The framework primarily makes a contribution to understanding intersections between gender and age. Examining youth peacebuilders' experiences across these different communities helps enhance understanding of the diverse ways gender may be represented and negotiated in a variety of settings, and how that might influence young people's experiences of and participation in violence and/or peacebuilding.

Integrating intersectionality: a plural, gender-inclusive approach to peace

Reflecting on gender or age alone is inadequate for understanding young people's lives and experiences.[22] Therefore, here we apply an intersectional analytic framework. This is a political choice, since intersectional approaches are insurgent, challenge the mainstream and highlight the limits of disciplines.[23] Intersectionality is not a standardised methodology or a grand theory, but rather an analytical tool or analytic disposition that can 'capture and engage contextual dynamics of power'.[24] Attention to intersectionality 'means that one always has to pay attention to specific contexts and their politics'.[25] Crucially, an intersectional analytic sensibility makes it possible to see and theorise intersecting axes of disadvantage (in this case gender and age). It emphasises structural and political inequalities while simultaneously allowing research to reveal the ways overlapping identity categories may be created and deployed.[26]

As indicated by our research and the broader range of research on youth peacebuilding it builds upon, it is clear that youth are not homogenous and their gendered experiences are not homogenous; for example, differences exist between different groups of boys as well as between different groups of girls. These differences

Dancing through the dissonance

are especially evident when it comes to stratification based on class and along the urban/rural divide. Indeed, other aspects of identity intersect with gender in constituting norms around violence and peace. As one Colombian interviewee explained:

> Here almost all men have to complete military service ... but if you study in university you can avoid that ... you can pay for your licence or military service, but if you are poor ... like 80 per cent of the population in Colombia, you have to do military service. Sometimes, if you live in Bogotá, you work in TransMilenio [public transport system], you have to stay all day long in a bridge or something ... but if you are from a rural area you have to be in the police station ... so if the guerrilla arrives in your town you have to fight them. There have been a lot of cases in which children ... men of 18 years or 19 years old are dead because they were doing military service. ('Camila', Colombia)

At the same time, legitimacy challenges appear particularly salient for young women working in peacebuilding, because of age, gender and language norms. As one of the young women in the US M4P programme told us:

> As a young person ... it's a matter of 'Okay, what language can I use to speak to people to legitimise these ideas?' ... They would assume that I was less capable ... then comes being a woman. I think that's difficult in ... legitimising my ideas ... because I think ... dance and emotional things ... are generally associated with female types and can be considered less legitimate because they are more emotional and less hard data ... In the context of [this programme] I think that being a female in that sense has influenced ... the language I use and ... motivation to legitimise my idea. ('Samantha', United States)

Overall, when it comes to conflict and violence, young people are affected, participate and respond in a range of ways influenced by both their age and other intersecting identity factors, such as gender. As Mies noted, hierarchical divisions between women and men inherently entwine with other social divisions, particularly where connections between gender- and age-based hierarchies are concerned.[27] For example, the UN Secretary-General's Youth Envoy has reported that young adult males account for an estimated 90 per cent of deaths from direct conflict, while young women globally comprise 10–30 per cent of armed groups. In conflict, meanwhile, adolescent girls are often disproportionately vulnerable to violence, exploitation and abuse, including physical and sexual abuse.[28] The same report notes that in conflict areas, less than half of youth are enrolled in secondary education, and for girls the number is substantially lower.

It is clear that gender significantly influences the everyday experiences of being young, so accounting for gender is crucial when looking at prospects for young people's participation in peace and security.[29] Both boys and girls are associated with women and represented as feminine compared to adult males,[30] yet girls may face particularly significant barriers to recognition and participation in peace and security initiatives.

Despite this, discussions of youth in peace and conflict tend to overlook gendered dimensions, using 'youth' or 'young people' to mean boys and young men. For example, research on children and armed conflict indicates that the issue of child soldiers has been dominant among advocacy networks. It has most often been represented by the image of an African boy, neglecting child soldiers who fall outside this stereotype, such as girls.[31] Boys and young men are often treated as an inherent security threat, even when they are attempting to flee conflict themselves.[32] At the same time, girls remain the most excluded group from peace processes and recognised political participation, and programmes aimed at youth tend to be male-dominated, while organisations for women are usually led by and aimed at older women.[33]

The programmes studied in this book are thus exceptional, given that the majority of their leaders are young women. What might we learn from them if we listen? And how might we analyse what we learn differently, depending on the lens we use? To explore these concerns, the remainder of this section discusses and explores an intersectional analysis of gender and age in the case studies, focusing on two key questions considered across all the sites: (1) how does gender impact youth participation in violence?, and (2) how does gender impact youth participation in peacebuilding? From there, a deeper exploration is provided of the broader question: how can the excluded be better included? In contemplating these questions, we illuminate key challenges and prospects when it comes to understanding gendered intersectionalities in youth peacebuilding.

How does gender impact youth participation in violence?

Young people in each of the case study sites were asked: 'Do you think young men or young women are more involved in conflict in your community, or do boys and girls get involved at the same rate? Why do you think that is?' In the US, all interviewees said boys were more physically violent, but many also said girls were as violent in different, non-physical ways. For example, one girl explained:

> If you are talking about physical violence, I would say boys; if you are talking about psychological violence ... it's equal, because I see the kinds of pressure ... girls put on other girls in their classes and in their social circles, and if you don't conform to what is deemed appropriate behaviour, then you are seriously attacked and abused in different ways. ('Olivia', United States)

In the Colombian and Philippines case studies, again, many said men and boys were more active in physical violence but that women and girls were involved in different ways. For example, 'Bea', a young woman from the Philippines, said: 'some of the boys in our community tend to cause conflict and violence. They easily get into trouble especially after alcohol intake.' Whereas, a young

Young people as peer leaders for peace

Colombian woman further explained: 'I think that they are equally involved but in a different way. The men are more involved in the direct violence – they are the people who shoot, the people who are in the FARC, in the guerrilla, and I think that the role of the men is more active.'

The programme's own studies also indicated that these views accurately described the situation of violence in the communities where the organisation worked. As two programme leaders told us:

> We do ... surveys ... looking at the type of violence that occurs in their school and a lot of times they answer with girls ... it's more like emotional and verbal violence and with the boys it's more physical violence. ('Emily', United States)

> We know that there are more boys and more men in the conflict than women, and the roles are clearly different in what they do in the armed groups ... we interviewed forty demobilised ex-combatants ... we were interested in understanding [the time before they were recruited] ... They [women] were doing exactly the same job, but at the same time, they were doing something different; women cooked, or they were sexual slaves ... the thing is that their participation is different. ('Isabela', Colombia)

Leaders in the US and Colombia also highlighted the need to avoid becoming too entrenched in generalisations, which can obscure differences within groups of girls and boys, including stereotyping girls as weak or ignoring the ways that women and girls can and do participate in physical violence, and/or are affected by violence perpetrated by men and boys.

Most interviewees in the US and Colombia, when asked why they felt men were more likely to be involved in physical violence and why women and girls were more likely to be violent in other ways, said it related to local cultural norms and expectations around how men and boys should behave as compared to women and girls. They highlighted how the pressure to follow gendered social norms could provoke or support violence for both boys and girls:

> I think it is socialisation. Girls ... use words as a weapon because we're taught physical aggression is less accepted in girls. ('Emma', United States)

> I feel like boys feel compelled to participate in physical violence and girls more in emotional violence and I think this has a lot to do with gender norms ... In order to not appear weak or ... feminine, a lot of boys assert themselves in a physically violent way, even when they don't really want to. ('Kaylee', United States)

> I think young men are more involved in direct violence because of sexism ... Here there are a lot of differences between men and women. ... You can see that in the careers ... in the household roles, in parenting ... I think women have more the role of the supporter, of being behind the war; they are the guerrillas' cooks. They accept the violence ... that is one of the ways in which they get involved. ('Camila', Colombia)

> In our country ... the boy is supposed to be more violent than the girl and the boy must be violent to ... win the girl. [These are] very complicated gender issues ... that we must work hard on, and that was not evident in the curriculum ... I think we should review the gender issue very carefully. ('Mateo', Colombia)

At the same time, two interviewees in the US explained that they felt the differences could be attributed to the fact that both boys and girls had different tools available to them for participating in conflict. They said this could be related to both physical differences and differences in social expectations. As one young woman explained:

> I hated to say that, but it's true ... most guys could kick my ass physically ... I'm not going to pick that fight ... But instead ... I do something that's ... more harmful in some way, like undercut someone socially or politically, destroy someone's reputation. ... I think that there's also like a fear ... I don't want to be hurt physically

> ... I feel like guys are less that way, or they're more interested in 'I could win that fight' versus 'what's going to happen to me?' I don't know if that's more socialised or it's something that's in their mind. ('Makayla', United States)

Similarly, in Colombia, one interviewee revealed that some of the reasons for entering the conflict were the same for both girls and boys:

> They are participating for the same kinds of reasons ... when they are not forced ... they enter because they have family, they need money ... Domestic violence ... is the number one reason for children going into the groups ... and love is another one ... That is a recruitment strategy ... let's say there is a small town somewhere and one of the guys from the armed group flirts and makes a woman fall in love and convinces her to go into the group ... that is very common to both sides. ('Isabella', Colombia)

Overall, across the different programme sites, gender norms had significant implications for how and why young people participated in, or were impacted by, violence. While these locations are very different, men and boys from all sites were expected to, and thus did, participate more often in physical violence than women and girls. Women and girls, however, were as active, taking on roles supporting conflict or participating in other forms of non-physical violence, which fit with the social expectations prescribed to their gender roles. While these gender-differentiated roles were evident in both locations, they also manifested in different ways, depending on local culture and other identity aspects, such as socioeconomic status.

How does gender impact youth participation in peacebuilding?

In the US, interviewees noted that women and girls were more likely to participate in activities like dance-based youth peacebuilding programmes, at least partly because – compared to men and boys – social norms suggested they were better suited to working with children, dancing, showing compassion and other emotions, and agreeing to group participation. Some leaders noted that this trend was context specific:

> [In] the US ... we say that we're coming from an equal footing with men, but there are ... statistics and studies that show that women are still at a disadvantage. Women still get paid less; there are less women CEOs ... Even though we have the choices ... there are still barriers to break in terms of being a leader and affecting change in our communities. But I think it's much more accessible in the US and in some countries than it is in others, so I guess it depends on the context. ('Emily', United States)

Other interviewees explained that the gendering of dance evolved with age, and the norms became more entrenched as time progressed. They said they felt that, in certain times and contexts, putting boys and girls together could lead to limited participation by one or the other, yet they also thought that these attitudes could be unlearned:

> Younger kids ... everyone is kind of just another kid, but when you get to fourth grade ... they're ... more aware of ... boys with boys, girls with girls ... it's like a hyperawareness, and so it seems that at that age they're more likely to segregate by gender. And I think that carries through middle school ... then in high school, depending on the context, sometimes you see ... a relaxing of the gender segregation. ('Emma', United States)

> I think at the middle-school level, boys and girls tend not to want to work with each other, but if you get them in groups by themselves, they will be ... much more likely to work and participate fully ... In general, in my experience, it's ... always been pretty equal that girls and boys have participated ... There have been situations where they won't work with each other ... for a lot of girls ... and boys

they are ... weirded out working with the opposite sex. ('Makayla', United States)

'Makayla' said she also felt that women were particularly aware of violence and the need to participate in peacebuilding due to often being targeted for gendered violence and facing inequalities themselves. Her reflections highlight the aspect of the gendered body being a site of physical violence while also embodying the potential for change. She thus said she felt particularly moved to participate as a woman but also to work to find ways to better involve men and boys in ending violence against women. She asserted:

> I'm definitely a feminist, and one of the things that bothers me the most in modern society is the inequalities between men and women ... or that violence against women is such a significant problem in our society and ... isn't discussed ... I think ... those things are at the heart of why I think peacebuilding is so important ... For me ... being a woman ... I understand what it means to be faced with these inequalities and ... I want to contribute to that dialogue. ... I ... think that there tends to be in the peacebuilding field more women than men, and I'm ... interested in figuring out how to bring more men to the table. Because ... issues with violence against women can't be fixed with men [who] are not passionate with that issue. ('Makayla', United States)

A few Colombian respondents noted their beliefs that women are more active in the field of peacebuilding. Just as work must be done to challenge gender norms that pressure men and boys not to participate in peacebuilding, or that particularly address violence against women and girls, work is also needed to ensure that women and girls' efforts at peacebuilding are supported and welcomed. Although social norms may point girls and women towards participating in 'soft' issues, challenges remain for broader social change at the level of formal politics and in wider circles of peacebuilding and negotiations that include primarily adults and men.

Colombian interviewees also suggested that it could be challenging for boys and girls to work together in particular circumstances:

> The school where we're working ... female friends are together. And ... because they are friends and some of the boys are there ... it's weird, you know. ('Sofia', Colombia)

Young women interviewed in the Philippines similarly noted:

> I noticed that there's more closeness to individuals of [the] same gender ... when we were grouped together ... girls were with girls and boys were with boys. We were sharing ideas but with the arrangement there [was] somewhat like [a] division between the two genders. Girls are comfortable with other girls as boys are comfortable with other boys. ('Sabina', Philippines)

> Since I'm teaching Grade 6, I can see the girls are much more timid or shy and then men are very confident in answering, participating. Even if I know that these girls are intelligent and they can do better than what they are showing, they are overcome by their shyness. ('Mirabelle', Philippines)

At the same time, interviewees in the Philippines tended to highlight their programme's approach to rejecting gender stereotypes or divisions:

> Each person has his own unique abilities. Gender is not a hindrance to leadership. It should be fair. ('Sabina', Philippines)

> In [M4P] we are not allowing gender rules. As [to] what I have [seen] or observed, our doings are more on building [a] friendly environment and [empathising] with other people so that we will be able to know what they have learned and know about their feelings. ('Jesza', Philippines)

Building on previous research, the responses in this section highlight key questions about gender segregation or integration in youth peacebuilding programmes and what balances and compromises can or should be made.[34] Such questions are important because responses in this study and others indicate that gender norms have a serious impact on whether and how boys and girls will participate in peacebuilding. This study indicates that, while young women may become active and take on leadership roles in such creative cultural programmes – as opposed to being the minority they are in most peace programmes – they still face many challenges to gaining legitimacy and respect for their work, as hierarchies based on both age and gender can situate their work as less 'serious' or 'important', than that of adults or boys. Boys can also face barriers to legitimacy due to age, and they may also feel limited in participating in peacebuilding when it is stereotyped as 'feminine' and thus deemed less appropriate for them. Furthermore, research has articulated a clear need to critically engage with inaccurate assumptions that young men cannot or do not also face vulnerabilities.[35] Noting this, we draw on and contribute to research aiming to move beyond essentialising gender dichotomies that foster stereotypical, oversimplified gendered notions of who might be seen as victims and/or perpetrators.[36]

How can the excluded be better included?

The question of how to create inclusive, gender-sensitive peacebuilding programmes is significant because even organisations working in good faith and with agreement can create injustices for their constituents. Richmond calls this a 'peace differend', as opposed to the liberal claim of the 'peace dividend'.[37] In youth peacebuilding programmes, a 'peace differend' may be evident if the initiative upholds, reifies or fails to challenge existing gender norms that promote exclusions and violence. Such gendered exclusions can occur even when programmes aim to use creative methods for peacebuilding.

Scholarship examining youth participation in community-based music programmes in Germany, Australia, the UK and the US has found that in most of the community youth music activities, few girls participate; though intended for all youth, eventually these programmes became appropriated as young men's domains. The researchers asked facilitators about girls' non-participation and how to address it. Some expressed the opinion that young men's domination was inevitable and could only be dealt with by single-sex activities, while others explained that some things, such as break dancing, are just more aligned with boys.[38] At least one said the problem was girls lacking interest or skills, which appears to be a common thread when explaining the exclusion of a particular group. Indeed, previous research has found that girls who participate in youth-led peacebuilding initiatives where young men dominate often face sexism. Non-participation by girls in these situations tends to be seen as a lack of interest or ability on the part of the girls rather than a structural failure to better accommodate them.[39] This parallels work in security studies, where threats linked to gender are often individualised and situated outside of the structural, political, public realm, and thus outside the bounds of consideration when seeking to build peace.[40] In contrast, the pursuit of positive peace requires questions to be asked about who might be left out and why, and how their exclusion might be addressed.

In the Philippines, M4P programming tended to be fairly gender balanced already. However, when facilitators in the US were asked how they would get more girls/boys to participate (if either were participating less), overwhelmingly the respondents suggested adapting the programme to address exclusions and to create a more welcoming and appealing environment for the excluded. At the same time, they said, care had to be taken to keep those who were already participating engaged. In particular, many asserted that the programme and its activities could be adapted to fit the interests of whoever was not participating, which in this case was most often boys:

> I think always connecting the material back to something that they're already interested in because … with … gender roles that are …

starting to be internalised or already are, dance is not something that boys do. ... So, finding a way that brings the activities in a way that ... it's not dance and ... also helping them learn that dance isn't just in pink and in ballet. ('Ashley', United States)

I... try to make references to things that are concerned [with] more male interest. Like I was talking about football today, and we talked a little bit about how different gestures that we have or different dance moves come from gestures that we use every day. ('Kaylee', United States)

In Colombia, again there was a tendency to identify a need to change the programme to better include young men:

Maybe a lot of boys are into sports like soccer, which is movement as well ... something that occurs to me is relating movement to sports. ('Alejandro', Colombia)

I think the idea of including more boys is something that goes beyond dance, is finding something they can relate [to] more, like a ball game, not necessarily football, but something they can relate to that still uses the body. ('Valeria', Colombia)

With this in mind, other participants highlighted the need to adapt to each gender as needed:

I think that for girls, communication is more important – you have to talk with them; you have to show them that they are important to you, because they are very shy and you have to be with them. ... You have to be always reminding them that they can do the things, that they are free ... With men, I think that they are more relaxed, with them I think that it's more important to do things all the time, because they get bored very easily ... with the boys it is a challenge to maintain ... focus on the topic. ('Camila', Colombia)

Moreover, although considerable discussion ensued around improving participation by using techniques that would appeal specifically to one gender, there was also discussion about how it is important to encourage young peacebuilders to step outside their comfort zones rather than adhering to existing norms. Some facilitators in the US said they felt this might occur by using small groups not based on existing friendship circles. At least one leader also suggested the need to directly and critically engage with the limiting aspects of gender norms in peacebuilding programmes:

> Ideally … I would work with a mixed gender and … if it's high school, then maybe you'll address that issue directly and speak about … those issues … in terms of dancing together. If one gender is less willing to participate than the other, then that would also speak to the levels of self-consciousness … I think one of the principles of the… curriculum that … is very important is that nothing is stupid. ('Samantha', United States)

A key aim was making the programme more inclusive. Some said this required challenging norms but also including same-sex role models:

> Colombia is still somewhat a sexist country so people believe that dance or choreography is for women, that if one speaks of a male dancer, then he is gay … I think that is one of the main problems we have, that boys think dancing … is for girls because that's what they have been taught, not because they truly believe it. The other problem is that we haven't had a lot of male facilitators; I think boys would feel more comfortable if it was men teaching them. ('Valeria', Colombia)

Social norms around gender were mentioned as limiting too, and interviewees also suggested the need to directly challenge existing gender norms in order to enhance gender equity in peacebuilding participation. This challenging of norms, though necessary, was also described as quite difficult to carry out. One key idea that emerged was the need to adapt the programme to fit the excluded while asking all participants to challenge norms that may lead to exclusion, including not alienating anyone for choosing not to participate in a given activity or at a given moment. As one young woman said:

> We can meet them at their boundaries. If you're not comfortable doing something you can make it so that … what you are comfortable with fits into the greater activity. … If a student is reluctant to dance … one of the tactics is that if someone is standing and crossing their arms [you say to them], 'Well, that is your move. That is your persona. And if you don't like that, you have to actually change it.' So, I don't think that the point is to point them out and say, 'Look at you, you're not dancing.' It's saying, 'Look at you, you are a part of this, whether you realise it or not. And if you want to participate, we're here to embrace you. And if you don't want to participate, we're not going to discriminate against that.' That is a huge part of building peace. ('Aubrey', United States)

In this way, she suggested that requesting instead of ordering participation and letting youth participants drive the programme could create a sense of welcome. Others also highlighted how important the act of welcoming or creating hospitable spaces for participation could be:

> If a student is upset about something … they can't participate … I would say, 'I'm so sorry that this isn't going the way you want it to,' or, 'Tell me what I can do to help,' or, 'What I can do to make it better?' … It's creating an open space for them to join you if they want to or an open space for them to not if they don't want to … I would say, 'Could you do me a really huge favour? This would really help me out a lot if you could work with him or her today.' … That helps you if you personalise it and you make it a request instead of an order. ('Makayla', United States)

The responses to key questions around gender indicate that dance can be useful in engaging youth in peacebuilding, but that it must be applied in sensitive, reflexive and culturally relevant ways to appeal to and include both young men and young women. Through highlighting the challenges and limitations gender norms place on young people when it comes to peacebuilding, the participants interviewed pointed to the need to create alternative pathways to support young men and young women in participating. Indeed, pursuing sustainable peace requires challenging existing norms around gender, age and other intersecting factors that sanction violence and hinder peacebuilding.

While masculine traits and ideas are often dominant in social spheres, including most youth peace programmes studied to date, looking at programmes where men and boys are a minority makes it possible to de-naturalise exclusion more readily, critically engaging with it and proposing new alternatives. The youth experiences documented here suggest that accounting for gender in the design, implementation and evaluation of youth peacebuilding programmes is both valuable and worthwhile. More specifically, as the young people cited here were quick to say, programmes ought to be adapted to fit boys if and when they are excluded; logically, the same extension of hospitality ought to apply to girls whenever they are marginalised. More broadly, as the youth participants in this study indicate, in contrast to efforts at 'fixing' those who might be excluded based on gender, youth peacebuilding programmes ought to be adapted to welcome the excluded.

Peer leadership for peace

Of course, any effort at peacebuilding depends both on who is included and who leads. Thus, while not wanting to essentialise any group of young people or people in general as 'naturally' disposed to doing a particular thing, including working with youth peacebuilders, it is worth noting that representation matters. Likewise, the fact that M4P was started by a young woman and, at the time this research was conducted, it continued to be run by

Young people as peer leaders for peace

that young woman, in all likelihood had an influence on its success in engaging youth, especially girls and young women, in peacebuilding. As one facilitator said of the programme:

> The fact that it was founded by a young woman ... [is] really inspirational ... for people that want to get involved ... and obviously her own desire [is crucial] to ... lift up women in their communities to empower other young women who want to ... make change in their communities. ('Emily', United States)

As this quote suggests, another key element that emerged from this research was the importance of peer leadership for peace. Existing research aimed at understanding and supporting youth leadership has featured increasing attention to youth-led programmes, such as those run by the organisation studied here.[41] However, the views of the young people involved in this research are especially illuminating in adding to the evidence base, since existing research on youth leadership rarely deals with peacebuilding or includes youth in settings facing conflict.[42]

The young people interviewed for this study reported that taking part in dance-based peacebuilding offered them an opportunity to teach, learn about and practise leadership in a variety of contexts. Indeed, although young people are often marginalised or excluded from leadership in peacebuilding efforts or politics more broadly, young leaders in this programme clearly articulated their views that youth can lead effectively.[43] As one interviewee noted:

> I don't think age imposes any limits. A person's interests or abilities, such as leadership, might affect that capacity but I don't think age is a restriction when it comes to peace development. ('Alejandro', Colombia)

Another facilitator expressed his view that leadership 'depends upon on how you manage yourself. If you think you can be a leader or a follower, then it can happen'. ('Jason', Philippines)

Not only can youth lead for peace, some suggested young people might even offer some unique insights, approaches or skills that may be less common in older leaders. This backs up previous research suggesting youth are often working to redefine or reimagine leadership in changing times.[44] As one facilitator expressed it:

> [When] the leader is [a] young man or [a] young woman then he/she would have fresh and new ideas. There's maybe a commitment in terms of his work and [being] more focused. While the older ones, they are committed to things like being married, engaged, or they have different responsibilities. ('Art', Philippines)

As his example suggests in referring to both young women and young men, observations and interviews in this research indicated that it is important to include people from different genders as leaders. The global organisation was also working towards the aim of diversifying the leadership of the organisation in terms of gender. The programme's founder and CEO stated that, at the time this research was conducted, she was

> definitely trying to recruit more boys, both [facilitators] and staff. It's a concern of mine in shaping the diversity of our leadership and the diversity of also our board. Like initially it was very women-heavy and now I think we have more men than women on our board.

These efforts link to previous research supporting the efficacy of leadership initiatives providing the chance for peer education from a diverse range of young people and other role models, and recognising and accounting for individual and structural factors that may influence young people's understandings and experiences of leadership.[45]

In the M4P programme, peer leaders from across the varied sites reported that engaging in this dance for peacebuilding initiative had helped them develop and practise their leadership skills, and had improved their capacity to mentor other young emerging peacebuilders and leaders. As Colombian facilitators explained:

> I think that [being part of M4P] reinforced my leadership ability. I'm normally a bit of an introvert, which is unusual given my line of work, but what's weird is that I switch roles in certain situations and I'm no longer the introvert I tend to be. Before I got to know dance and psychology, I was a very isolated person. Dancing helped me get out into the world, so I think the programme reinforced my leadership skills through the strategies it used. ('Alejandro', Colombia)

> I think that [M4P] helped me to improve my leadership skills and group management skills, which I think is very important. ('Camila', Colombia)

Young leaders for peace in the American programme sites also stated that dance had helped them develop leadership skills:

> I mean, personally, dance for me taught me a whole lot … and I learned so much just about leadership and about myself and about working with other people. ('Kaylee', United States)

They also noted that this goes beyond peer leaders to include leadership development for the programme participants:

> It gets students to get involved, and it really turns students into leaders, and maybe it will get students into student government because they became interested in [M4P], or they can look at how to help their community because they became involved in [M4P], or coming up with new idea or project. ('Makayla', United States)

Finally, another young leader in M4P noted that the programme was designed to foster peer mentoring and progression in leadership development:

> We have this progressive pipeline curriculum that means pre-K through twelfth grade, the idea is that in high school we have the

junior [M4P facilitator] model where we're fostering mentorship opportunities where they can mentor lower grade students and be mentored by our [M4P facilitators]. And then leadership opportunities where they can [gain] experience to teach past lessons learned to students in lower grades. So, the context of mentorship and leadership is really important to us and finding ways that they can stay engaged and to broaden the peacebuilding process but also the [M4P] family – like we tell them, once you're a part of [M4P], you're a forever part of the [M4P] global network. ('Emma', United States)

When it comes to leadership for peace, the peer leaders involved in this research demonstrated their beliefs that young people can effectively lead for peace, and they can even bring new and unique insights, skills and resources to peacebuilding. They further understood dance to be a relevant and accessible way to engage young people, not only in peacebuilding but also in developing a capacity for leadership in peacebuilding and beyond. Finally, they emphasised the importance of including a diverse range of actors in leadership opportunities, of supporting peer leaders and of having experienced youth mentor other youth peacebuilders.

Conclusion

Overall, this chapter has taken important steps in preparing the groundwork for understanding the thematic chapters that follow. It explored the role of young people as peer leaders and how dance facilitated peacebuilding in the case studies we considered. By providing a contextual background to each site, including the important ways in which the factors of gender and age intersect in these contexts, we hope the reader will be able to think critically through the remaining chapters, considering similarities and differences, not only across different locations for peacebuilding but also across the experiences of different individuals, communities and groups in the different sites.

Notes

1 United Nations, 'UN Charter' (San Francisco: United Nations, 26 June 1945), full text available at: www.un.org/en/sections/un-charter/un-charter-full-text/ (accessed 18 October 2019).
2 H. W. Jeong, *Peacebuilding in Postconflict Societies: Strategy and Process* (Boulder: Lynne Rienner, 2005); L. J. Pruitt, *Youth Peacebuilding: Music, Gender, and Change* (Albany: State University of New York (SUNY) Press, 2013).
3 E. Porter, 'Women, political decision-making, and peace-building', *Global Change, Peace and Security*, 15 (2003), pp. 245–62.
4 Office of the Secretary-General's Envoy on Youth, '#YouthStats: armed conflict' (New York: United Nations, 2016), p. 3.
5 T. A. Borer, J. Darby and S. McEvoy-Levy, *Peacebuilding After Peace Accords: The Challenges of Violence, Truth, and Youth* (Notre Dame: University of Notre Dame Press, 2006); J. P. Lederach, *The Moral Imagination: The Art and Soul of Building Peace* (Oxford: Oxford University Press, 2005); S. McEvoy-Levy, 'Youth as social and political agents: issues in post-settlement peace building', Kroc Institute Occasional Paper #21:OP:2 (Notre Dame: Kroc Institute's Research Initiative on the Resolution of Ethnic Conflict, 2001); S. Schwartz, *Youth and Post-Conflict Reconstruction: Agents of Change* (Washington DC: United States Institute of Peace Press, 2010); A. M. S. Watson, 'Can there be a "Kindered" peace?', *Ethics and International Affairs*, 22 (2008), pp. 35–42.
6 Watson, 'Can there be a "Kindered" peace?'.
7 A. Harris, *Young People and Everyday Multiculturalism* (New York and London: Routledge 2013), p. 143.
8 A. Özerdem, S. Podder and E. L. Quitoriano, 'Identity, ideology and child soldiering: community and youth participation in civil conflict – a study on the Moro Islamic Liberation Front in Mindanao, Philippines', *Civil Wars*, 12 (2010), p. 317.
9 Pruitt, *Youth Peacebuilding*.
10 C. Sylvester, 'Empathetic cooperation: a feminist method for IR', *Millennium: Journal of International Studies*, 23 (1993), pp. 315–34.
11 B. A. Ackerly, M. Stern and J. True, 'Conclusion', in *Feminist Methodologies for International Relations*, ed. by B. A. Ackerly, M. Stern and J. True (Cambridge: Cambridge University Press, 2006), p. 259; C. Enloe, *The Curious Feminist: Searching for Women in a New Age of Empire* (Berkeley: University of California Press, 2004); J. A. Tickner, *Gendering World Politics: Issues and Approaches in the Post-Cold War Era* (New York: Columbia University Press, 2001); J. A. Tickner, *Gender in International Relations: Feminist Perspectives on Achieving Global Security* (New York: Columbia University Press, 1992), p. 40.
12 O. P. Richmond, 'Reclaiming peace in international relations', *Millennium: Journal of International Studies*, 36 (2008), pp. 439–70.

13 *Ibid.*; H. Berents, 'From the margins: conflict-affected young people, social exclusion, and an embodied everyday peace in Colombia' (PhD thesis, University of Queensland, 2013).
14 V. Jabri, *War and the Transformation of Global Politics* (London: Palgrave, 2007).
15 C. Zelizer and R. A. Rubinstein, eds, *Building Peace: Practical Reflections from the Field* (Sterling: Kumarian Press, 2009).
16 L. J. Pruitt, 'Gendering the study of children and youth in peacebuilding', *Peacebuilding*, 3 (2015), pp. 157–70.
17 L. J. Pruitt, 'The women, peace and security agenda: Australia and the agency of girls', *Australian Journal of Political Science*, 49 (2014), pp. 486–98.
18 H. Berents, 'An embodied everyday peace in the midst of violence', *Peacebuilding*, 3 (2015), pp. 1–14; Borer, Darby and McEvoy-Levy, *Peacebuilding After Peace Accords*; K. Huynh, B. d'Costa, and K. Lee-Koo, *Children and Global Conflict* (Cambridge: Cambridge University Press, 2015); McEvoy-Levy, 'Youth as social and political agents'; A. McIntyre and T. Thusi, 'Children and youth in Sierra Leone's peace-building process', *African Security Review*, 12 (2003), https://doi.org/10.1080/10246029.2003.9627222; Pruitt, *Youth Peacebuilding*; Schwartz, *Youth and Post-Conflict Reconstruction*.
19 H. Berents and L. J. Pruitt, 'Not just victims or threats: young people win recognition as workers for peace', *The Conversation* (16 December 2015), available at https://theconversation.com/not-just-victims-or-threats-young-people-win-recognition-as-workers-for-peace-52284 (accessed 18 October 2019).
20 UNDP, 'Youth strategy 2014–2017: empowered youth, sustainable future' (New York: United Nations Development Programme, 2014), p. 47.
21 AUC, 'African youth charter' (Banjul: African Union Commission, 2006).
22 This section of the chapter incorporates some excerpts of material previously published in Pruitt, 'Gendering the study of children and youth in peacebuilding'.
23 S. Cho, K. W. Crenshaw and L. McCall, 'Toward a field of intersectionality studies: theory, applications, and praxis', *Signs: Journal of Women and Culture in Society*, 38 (2013), p. 793.
24 *Ibid.*, p. 798.
25 A. T. R. Wibben, 'Introduction: feminists study war', in *Researching War: Feminist Methods, Ethics and Politics*, ed. by A. T. R. Wibben (Abingdon and New York: Routledge, 2016), p. 22.
26 Cho, Crenshaw and McCall, 'Toward a field of intersectionality studies', p. 797.
27 M. Mies, *Patriarchy and Accumulation on a World Scale: Women in the Division of Labour* (London: Zed Books, 2014).
28 Office of the Secretary-General's Envoy on Youth, '#YouthStats: armed conflict'.

29 H. Brocklehurst, *Who's Afraid of Children? Children, Conflict and International Relations* (London: Ashgate, 2006).
30 Ibid., p. 163.
31 K. Lee-Koo, 'Horror and hope: (re)presenting militarised children in global North–South relations', *Third World Quarterly*, 32 (2011), pp. 725–42. For an important work that does engage with girls as child soldiers, see C. Coulter, *Bush Wives and Girl Soldiers: Women's Lives through War and Peace in Sierra Leone* (Ithaca: Cornell University Press, 2009).
32 L. J. Pruitt, H. Berents and G. Munro, 'Gender and age in the construction of male youth in the European "migration crisis"', *Signs: Journal of Women and Culture in Society*, 43 (2018), pp. 687–709.
33 M. Sommers, 'Fearing Africa's young men: male youth, conflict, urbanization, and the case of Rwanda', in *The Other Half of Gender: Men's Issues in Development*, ed. by I. Bannon and M. Correia (Washington DC: The World Bank, 2006), pp. 137–58.
34 L. J. Pruitt, '"Fixing the girls": neoliberal discourse and girls' participation in peacebuilding', *International Feminist Journal of Politics*, 15 (2013), pp. 58–76.
35 P. Schulz, 'The "ethical loneliness" of male sexual violence survivors in Northern Uganda: gendered reflections on silencing', *International Feminist Journal of Politics*, 20 (2018), pp. 583–601.
36 C. Dolan, 'Has patriarchy been stealing the feminists' clothes? Conflict-related sexual violence and UN Security Council resolutions', *IDS Bulletin*, 45 (2014).
37 Richmond, 'Reclaiming peace in international relations', p. 455.
38 S. Baker and B. M. Z. Cohen, 'From snuggling and snogging to sampling and scratching: girls' nonparticipation in community-based music activities', *Youth and Society*, 39 (2008), pp. 316–39.
39 Pruitt, '"Fixing the girls"'.
40 L. Hansen, 'The Little Mermaid's silent security dilemma and the absence of gender in the Copenhagen School', *Millennium: Journal of International Studies*, 29 (2000), pp. 285–36.
41 N. Blanchet-Cohen and L. Brunson, 'Creating settings for youth empowerment and leadership: an ecological perspective', *Child and Youth Services*, 35 (2014), pp. 216–36; J. J. Bulanda *et al.*, '"Keeping it real": an evaluation audit of five years of youth-led program evaluation', *Smith College Studies in Social Work*, 83 (2013), pp. 279–302; J. Connolly *et al.*, 'Evaluation of a youth-led program for preventing bullying, sexual harassment, and dating aggression in middle schools', *Journal of Early Adolescence*, 35 (2015), pp. 403–34; M. Delgado and L. Staples, *Youth-Led Community Organizing: Theory and Action* (New York: Oxford University Press, 2008).
42 L. J. Pruitt, 'Youth leadership: an annotated bibliography' (London: PLAN International, 2017); J. Ungerleider, 'Structured youth dialogue to

empower peacebuilding and leadership', *Conflict Resolution Quarterly*, 29 (2012), pp. 381–402.
43 M. Chou *et al.*, *Young People, Citizenship and Political Participation: Combatting Civic Deficit?* (Lanham: Rowman & Littlefield, 2017).
44 J. Mortensen *et al.*, 'Leadership through a youth lens: understanding youth conceptualizations of leadership', *Journal of Community Psychology*, 42 (2014), pp. 447–62; J. Mortensen, 'An empirical investigation of an emerging youth-driven model of leadership: the Collective Change Youth Leadership Framework' (PhD thesis, Michigan State University, 2016).
45 Pruitt, 'Youth leadership'.

3
Local/global dance 'hubs' for peace

> *I think the great thing about our curriculum is that we contextualise what we do in each locale based on the needs of the community because [M4P] Philippines, though they're using the same curriculum as [M4P] New York City and [M4P] Bogotá, [M4P] Baltimore, the curriculum, as you saw, the training is very organic, very driven by the participants. So, they create their own movements. They drive where the programme goes. We provide them with the framework for that peace[building] process. So, it really is localised to their needs.*
>
> 'Claire', M4P founder, United States

Do local actors working outside the Global North experience and perceive the M4P process as localised? And what does it mean to be localised when it comes to peacebuilding programming? In this chapter we investigate what dance and creative movement can tell us about local and/or global approaches to peacebuilding, including how the local and the global are defined, interact or may co-constitute one another, including in relation to peacebuilding. To that end, this chapter reflects on participant statements around 'local' and 'global' themes to highlight the complexity of these overlapping spheres when it comes to peacebuilding. We suggest that, while these spheres may not be as dichotomous as they are often presented, taking care to reflect on these concepts is important to peacebuilding, since they often have a strong resonance with those living in conflict-affected settings. After all, as Lederach points out, when things are removed from people, they feel foreign and may thus be less effective:

> When things happen, locally or nationally, and people do not have a sense of touch and feel, the distance expands and they feel removed and remote. Correspondingly, the processes are perceived as foreign and unconnected, creating a sense of imposition, or, worse, apathy.[1]

Keeping this in mind, it is significant here that the key participants in this research project are youth, since, although it has only just begun to be well recognised, 'Young people are key stakeholders in peace and security efforts'.[2] The early part of the twenty-first century has seen an increased focus on youth in global political discourse, including that of key international aid and development programmes, such as those hosted by the UN and the World Bank, among others.[3] Although such attention has only constituted early steps towards addressing young people's continued marginalisation in peacebuilding, it is clear that 'young people can and do participate in peacebuilding, including through creative work to build cultures of peace locally, nationally, regionally, and globally'.[4]

An examination of the roles youth play in peacebuilding can offer insights into constructions of and connections between the local and global. Engaging with these insights may even transform the ways peacebuilders understand peace, including our capacity to understand it through creative practices, such as dance and creative movement. In taking young peacebuilders' experiences seriously, this chapter considers the creation and sharing of 'hub dances' – group dance exchange activities across and between programme sites – and it simultaneously examines the political ramifications of this co-creation and/or interchange. Hub dances are envisioned to serve as a vehicle for cross-cultural moments of exchange and to provide opportunities for (re)creating identities in ways that can support peacebuilding.

Considering hub dances also facilitates examination of the different cultural contexts in which conflict occurs. In particular, looking at hub dances highlights tensions around possibilities that the homogenisation of dance could foster stereotypes, while also suggesting prospects for presenting and understanding identities through dance in ways that foster acceptance of or even valuing of differences. Likewise, we consider the ways in which the creation, practice and exchange of hub dances enacts meaning around identity for self, others and the community, and how this relates to the creation of broader social change for peacebuilding.

Where or what is the local, the global? What does that mean for a politics of peace?

By making bodies central in our theorising, we are able to identify and generate new ways of thinking about global political dynamics, including in ways that can point to new directions for politics.[5] Our findings from the case studies suggest prospects for new understandings of 'the local' and 'the global', and point to the need to make space for complex understandings that encompass and create a wider variety of scales for enacting a politics of peace. After all, just as the body may be another scale for understanding 'below' the level of the local, the local can also be understood as mutually constitutive with the personal as well as the global.[6]

In considering scales in relation to peacebuilding, we initially focus on the concept of 'operational scale', which locates the level at which patterns and processes operate.[7] At the same time, we do not take scale as a given or as situated within some predetermined hierarchical arrangement from local to regional to national and global, but rather as a dependent result of tensions between human agents' actions and structural dynamics.[8] As Smith explains: 'There is nothing ontologically given about the traditional division between home and locality, urban and regional, national and global scales.'[9] Instead, scales are relational, with differentiation established through the geographical structure and (re)production of social interactions and political processes.[10]

Drawing on insights from human geography scholars, we envision scale to be socially constructed and also implicated in the ways space is socially produced and thus political.[11] Scale is 'not socially or politically neutral, but embodies and expresses power relationships'.[12] Constructing scale is likewise seen here as an ongoing, contested and dynamic political process that may also be open to transformation.[13] Different understandings of scale define and shape varied ideological and political positions while also outlining perceptions of lived experience.[14] Nevertheless, it is important to acknowledge that the ways scale is produced also have tangible, material outcomes, as seen in the experiences of M4P participants.[15]

We accept that 'the local and the global are mutually constituted', and other spatial scales also heavily influence this process and explanations for significant occurrences with global, local and national consequences.[16] In many ways, the local and the global are identified, modified and remain fluid through their relation with each other.[17] Movement to the global or the local does not inherently increase the validity of one perspective, but rather emphasises the social-spatial relationship that is continually regenerated and redefined.[18] These changing conceptualisations of scale can empower some while disempowering others, expressing alterations to social power as influential ways for ordering political processes.[19]

Critical peacebuilding research has highlighted 'the entangled quality of local and global normative discourses',[20] suggesting that a global construction of the local and a local construction of the global coexist.[21] Recognising this, it remains important to hear non-elite narratives alongside dominant discourses.[22] International organisations have started to take the need for local ownership of development more seriously, simultaneously increasing broad acknowledgement of the value of 'the local' in IR and development studies.[23]

Including and valuing local discourses increases the complexity of the choreography of local and global actors. This complexity is evident as these actors move to navigate different approaches to peacebuilding, including questions of who leads or follows in diverse contexts in which neither the local nor the global are fixed or universally understood. Concepts of hybridity have been proposed as one approach to understand how localised authority operates in ways that may collaborate with top-down approaches.[24] Yet, the local can also be implemented as a myth, often uncritically valorised by major development actors at the global level while being deployed to legitimate actions and approaches that may nonetheless originate from outside global actors.[25] Under this unreflective, uncritical laudatory paradigm, 'the local is assumed to be better than any alternative'.[26] It can be challenging to operate outside global norms when key global actors have deemed the local as the preferred site and foundation of the authentic.[27] After all, often those working in development at the 'local', 'national' or 'regional' level are engaged in ongoing relationships with Western organisations regarding funding and norms.[28] Adding further complexities, the global has its own sense of 'local', which emerges in our case studies from localities of the urban centres in the US in that an NGO's office can simultaneously be local, national or global at the same time, depending on participant perspectives.[29] Nonetheless, Anderl suggests that 'the global discursive shift towards the local' may offer some emancipatory power, though it may be limited.[30]

While the terms 'local' and 'global' remain messy and contested, and thus subject to critique, in our research the centrality of these terms among participants' remarks and programme frameworks leaves us convinced that they require further exploration. Understanding both visible and hidden local/global relationships has clear implications for peacebuilders seeking to enact transformative politics more broadly, including across varied political scales.

As Cox explains, in understanding local politics it is worth acknowledging the ways in which the local may be embedded in processes taking place at different levels of reality and abstraction.[31] Political actors can also exploit linkages between the global and the local; moreover, local groups not entirely contained by the market or the local state can take part in producing place and can connect to different scales other than the local.[32] Finally, 'to the extent that oppositional movements can move across scales – that is, to the extent that they can take advantage of the resources at one scale to overcome the constraints encountered at different scales in the way that more powerful actors can do – they may have greater potential for pressing their claims'.[33]

Through creating space for alternative conceptualisations, the local, even when it functions in a rhetorical or mythical capacity, may be taken up by large global agencies with a claim to support local ownership. In doing so, '[t]hese processes may disrupt the current global discourse on what it means to develop'.[34] What might be the implications for this when it comes to community development efforts aimed at peacebuilding? And when considering peacebuilding efforts, is 'to scale or not to scale' a local or a global question?

In pursuit of a peace that's local, global or beyond?

Traditionally, international peacebuilding has existed as a massive social engineering experiment involving the grafting of Western models for organising the world in political, social and economic ways onto conflict-affected states with the aim of controlling civil conflict – 'in other words, pacification through political and economic liberalization'.[35] Likewise, models created by international experts travel around the world, landing in agencies, governments and NGOs where they are 'decoded and re-coded'.[36] In this context, internationally developed toolkits have been repeatedly deployed in a top-down fashion in varied local or national settings of conflict and have dominated peacebuilding efforts.[37] Criticising this approach in the international peace industry, Paris theorised that it would not foster sustainable peace but could instead actually fuel existing or future conflicts.[38]

Local/global dance 'hubs' for peace

In the face of such critiques, increasingly the local has been deemed central to peace.[39] Under this paradigm shift, promoted by John Paul Lederach, Kevin Avruch and others, top-down approaches to peace created in the West have been questioned, and focus has shifted towards local actors and human security as opposed to traditional military security.[40] In this early local turn, the aim was to support locals to increase their capacity for peace-building, while in a later local turn, supported by Mac Ginty and Richmond, among others, the local has often been positioned as autonomous, particular and resistant to liberal international actors.[41]

Such work 'distances itself from the enforcement of external models and top-down approaches and moves the "local" and "culture" into the centre of attention and action', adopting and mobilising 'local social and cultural capital for peace'.[42] For example, MacLeod emphasises sensitivity to local input alongside external evaluation.[43] A key idea here is, as Anderson and Olson suggest: 'No one can make anyone else's peace';[44] thus, ideally, 'peace and reconciliation initiatives should be conducted by locals themselves, non-local actors only acting as facilitators, if at all'.[45]

However, achieving this ideal is not without its challenges, especially given the often highly inequitable power relations between local and global actors, as well as between different local actors. Buckley-Zistel frames these frictional spaces between local and global as creative moments of connectivity.[46] As such, 'imagination is required to engage in the difficult "politics of translation" that transnational encounters inevitably entail',[47] and this imagination must be found on both sides of the scalar equation. The possibility for exchange exists if actors are ready to listen, value local knowledge, engage in self-reflection and take on challenges to their own norms, values and worldviews.[48]

While Bräuchler suggests that international peacebuilders coming from 'outside' need to be careful when dealing with local initiatives, to avoid taking away ownership and thus legitimacy,[49] it is important to note that these dichotomies of local versus global and inside versus outside are not always clear-cut. After all, peacebuilders participate in a range of interconnected cultures, and 'are constantly (re)negotiating modes of belonging and questions of identity, in times of peace and conflict'.[50] Richmond thus suggests a 'detailed understanding (rather than co-option or "tolerance") of local culture, traditions, and ontology'.[51]

The local turn in peacebuilding has situated culture as crucial to understanding peace, conflict and security, but the dominant disciplines involved in Peace and Conflict Studies have struggled to grasp the local, given the primacy of quantitative frameworks and solutionist approaches.[52] Even though 'local ownership' was intended to mean that peacebuilding would be planned, owned and carried out at the local level, peacebuilding efforts lauded under this banner have often instead been created and 'imposed on affected communities by outside actors'.[53]

Meanwhile, this turn to the local has often ignored heterogeneity at the local level or has functioned as empty rhetoric.[54] In such cases, the 'local' and 'culture' are depicted in a stereotypical fashion, seen as inherently positive or negative, harmonious or disorderly, and reflecting values that do not adhere to liberal standards.[55] While relying on these inaccurate tropes, research on local cultures has commonly been instrumentalised to suggest cultural sensitivity in interventions, counterinsurgency or conflict resolution processes.[56] In some of the worst cases, culture has been manipulated and instrumentalised to serve not the cause of peace, but of genocide, nation building, colonialism or the 'War on Terror'.[57]

Here we agree with Bräuchler that neither local mechanisms, nor international approaches for that matter, are inherently positive;[58] they can promote peace, but they can also trigger new conflict; they can be exclusionary, just as they can be inclusive. Indeed, we can see how local cultural concepts need not only to be understood, but may at times also require reimagining or reinterpreting in the pursuit of peace.[59] It then emerges that 'the question is not primarily whether certain cultural elements have actually been invented or

Local/global dance 'hubs' for peace

introduced from the outside in the (colonial) past, but whether and for what reason they are important to current negotiation processes'.[60]

While approaches labelled 'local' may at times be idealised in development and peacebuilding discourse, critical engagement is needed, particularly given that, along with international actors or government officials, local elites can also hijack processes to serve their own interests or to prevent addressing structural issues that may underlie causes of the conflict at hand.[61] Bräuchler asserts that the aim is not 'to idealise tradition, but to identify shared and integrative cultural values and norms that provide enough space to allow for cultural difference in each individual group'.[62] After all, looking closely at the local reveals a constructed heterogeneity that subsumes a variety of interests and actors. Within each 'local' group there can be nuances of diversity that may be overshadowed in representations that are generated for external groups. One of our participants from Colombia, 'Mateo', explained that within M4P, diversity tended to be understood as accounting for differences between different countries in the world. Yet, from his perspective, more attention is needed to account for diversity within different countries in the world. For example, he pointed to the need to 'understand that in Colombia there are Afro-Indigenous' people, who ought to be considered when adjusting the programmes to include a diverse range of participants. In other words, as Seyla Benhabib points out, just as communication across cultures involves difference, every culture also features ongoing contestation of its own narratives.[63] In short, countries or cultures should not be treated as internally homogeneous – taking a homogenised, fixed approach to 'the local' and culture could reify the dominance of one group and, in doing so, exclude others, for example migrants or indigenous peoples. To prevent such possible bases for conflict, it is important to look not only at local structures, beliefs and practices, but also at national policy frameworks that may have effects at local levels. It is thus, where possible, crucial that the State not be 'let off the hook' even while noting the important roles that citizens and residents can play in informal political efforts at peace. Overall, local culture, including custom, can be understood as fluid and ever evolving, and also as a potential source for creating peaceful futures tied to a sense of place, community and history.

Local young people pursuing global peace?

Here we suggest that our understandings of local and global, and indeed concepts of scale more broadly, can be aided by considering the perspectives of young people who are actively negotiating these concepts in their lived realities. The lives of youth are particularly relevant when exploring local and global dimensions of peace. According to Anita Harris, the generation of people experiencing youth in the early twenty-first century has distinctive resources to engage in building connections, including those constructed transnationally and virtually; moreover, she says, contemporary young people often take part in forging dynamic, inclusive community arrangements that are heterogeneous, unpredictable, porous and contested.[64] These characteristics of youth were certainly evident in this research. At the same time, our aim is not to offer some idealised framing of youth, as with related terms of 'local' or 'culture', but like Harris, to better understand young people's experiences and views in all their complexity.

The same goes for understanding discourses around and representations of youth, as these are also political and influence policy and practice. Indeed, certain key discourses relating to youth tend to frame policy at the global level. These are: '(1) children have rights and should be protected; (2) youth are a development asset; (3) youth are a threat to security; and (4) youth are agents of change'.[65]

All of these discourses have their limitations. For example, while many have advocated for popularising the notion of 'youth as agents of peace' in conflict zones, this has sometimes resulted in retaliation by elites or elders who benefit from the current status quo, or in youth being disappointed at the failure to meet such raised expectations.[66] As such, even this seemingly benign lens shows how such discourses are limited as they can oversimplify youth or result in their exploitation.[67] At the same time, no organisation acts in a way that follows a single one of these discourses without deviating from it; indeed, within and between actors and organisations, such influential ideas about young people can be manipulated, politicised and challenged.[68]

Moreover, while these key ideas shape global policy and global debates, locally, in countries affected by conflict, ideas about youth both mirror such discourses and deviate from them.[69] For example, in varied settings youth may be deemed a radical frontline, custodians of morality, dishonourable brutes and, in some sites, as a mixture of these archetypes and others over time.[70] At the national or local level, youth and children hold emotional significance that is not encompassed by global frameworks. As such they may be deemed to embody national anguish or existential threat, the nation's achievement or optimism in the future, or be deployed symbolically in support of continuing aggression or in pursuing peace.[71] Based on this range of discourses, youth may offer insights on how we understand where and how peace can or does occur.

The young people involved in our research across the three case study sites helped shed light on their views, which included space for complexity, such as the commonly held view among them that, like violence, peace exists on a spectrum that includes various levels or scales, involving global, local, others and self, and that 'peace' functions as both an inner state and an action word. In other words, in the view of youth, peace crosses the scales of local and global, and it also moves beyond and between them. For example, as M4P's founder explained when asked for her understandings of what peace means:

> What I like about [M4P] is that it is connecting up from the schools, the communities, the global level. That it [is] all interrelated ... it

started with first inner peace. And then we work towards community-level peace and then eventually global peace … students in the Bronx, who would not otherwise be able to feel like global citizens and global leaders because they've never even been into Manhattan, are able to connect with kids without having to learn a different language and look [to] different … kids in Latin America or kids in Europe who are also working towards this common goal to end violence, to transform conflict in their community. ('Claire', M4P founder, United States)

In this way, the youth involved tended to describe peace as originating at the smallest, most proximate level and moving outward to eventually affect the broader world. This process of starting with the self and radiating outwards may reflect a sense of individual agency within the larger networks of actors.[72] However, as we discuss later, making connections with global actors through M4P was also seen as valuable in a variety of ways.

Moreover, as discussed in more detail in other chapters, research participants also noted that there are limits to scaling; peace takes time and cannot be achieved by a one-off short-term project in a single site. Rather, they explained, peace has to be an ongoing process that includes consistent efforts, negotiations and processes that cover an array of spheres, including, but not limited to, policies, actions, schools, families, communities, media and culture. At the same time, participants noted the importance of both literally and figuratively translating models and information in the programme:

> I think another area where we need to improve is making our programme and tailoring our facilitation models so that it's accessible to English language learners, people who don't speak English very well; in Colombia, people who don't speak Spanish but speak indigenous languages. Also, framing what [M4P] is, and what it is not – I think we could do some more with that. I think we are at a place where people are saying, 'I think [M4P] is really cool, could you focus on XYZ?' and we'll sort of make the adaptation. There

needs to be a time where we say, '[M4P] is this, and not that' … so, what are those boundaries, and how do we control them? ('Makayla', United States)

The participants expressed the desire to translate materials, both linguistically and culturally, but also to be involved in decision-making about what the parameters of the programme would be in their local setting. Overall, we aspire to support a plural peace built on aesthetic politics. We understand this to include work incorporating multiple understandings and experiences of peace while encouraging creative engagement across difference. Likewise, in our research, we consider whether local approaches may be transposed in other local settings, whether they might be co-opted or instrumentalised by outside actors, and/or whether local actors might be offering innovative solutions in their context that may also apply in other settings.

It is important to recognise that young people's views of themselves will always be more complex than global, national or local ideas or trends can account for.[73] After all, as research has shown, a variety of factors – such as intergenerational dynamics, gender and class – influence young people's interpretations of who is or can be seen as a 'youth' and what challenges they might face.[74] Across these spheres '[l]ocal-level framing also matters', not least because local understandings about young people can be altered or adapted in the face of conflict or violence, which can influence meanings in ways that impact prospects for peace.[75] Moreover, as some participants in our study explained, 'local' approaches that are more generalised may not account for particular needs or interests of young people:

> [When] we were modifying or reviewing [the Colombian country leader]'s curriculum, before going to Cuba, we realised that [it] is very important [to have] a general curriculum, but also you need to generate conceptualised curriculums. [By] conceptualised I refer to a specific culture and ages or generations. ('Luciana', Colombia)

In this way, Luciana shows how important it is to reflect on and find space for diversity, including between ages or generations when trying to 'localise' efforts for peace. The concept of 'translating' approaches to peace more broadly across the different case study sites came up again and again as a key aspiration of the global organisation. The emphasis on translation within context highlights the importance of vernacular influences and how localised factors can shape ideas of safety or community.[76] This presents a major challenge in relation to local ownership or contextual 'fit' and also serves as a potentially productive area for supporting and linking young people in their quest for building peace across a variety of scales.

Many participants across the programme sites explained that they felt the global curriculum, which was developed in the 'local' context of the US, could and should be better developed to specific contexts elsewhere. For example, as the then Latin American director explained:

> It's like I have to Colombianise or Latin Americanise the programme ... so any time that I have to Colombianise that, [it] is like I'm putting part of myself in the programme and the programme is getting all this Colombian structure and Latin American structure. ('Sofia', Colombia)

Another of her fellow peer leaders in Colombia highlighted how further work should be ongoing with the aim of better adjusting the curriculum to fit the community. Reflecting on his last experience with the programme, he told us:

> The curriculum that I knew was a very gringo curriculum ... One important suggestion is that every curriculum should be worked on and built with the community [where] you are working. I think [it's] something crazy to bring a [programme] from elsewhere to implement in a community that has its own dynamics and how they see, think and feel different from elsewhere. I think this is hard work to do. Obviously, it's interesting to have a matrix management model of

Local/global dance 'hubs' for peace

how the curriculum works, but to me the curriculum is built with the community that you are going to work in and [not] imposed from another community. ... I think we should include all these factors ... that our country is also memory, is history ... [In] our country, there is [so] much impunity, in our country there are issues [that are] very, very important and relevant that people should know. ('Mateo', Colombia)

Moreover, when discussing what it means to be Colombian, and exploring understandings and experiences of violence and peace in that context, many young Colombians suggested that the outside view of their country could often focus on problems and challenges without giving adequate attention to the strengths Colombians might possess, or without adequately accounting for the love many held for their country and the responsibility they felt for contributing to building peace there and beyond. For some, this was in part based in their sense of '*hechar para adelante*', a maxim which one young Colombian woman described as 'so Colombian', in reflecting a sense of moving forward, doing things to successful completion, not being caught in the past or carrying on in a difficult situation.

When asked their thoughts on whether there might be any way to improve the M4P programme, several young people in the Philippines also pointed to the need for more effective localisation of the programme to their context:

We have different perspective[s] on how to make this organisation grow but as I experienced ... the curriculum is American, so I think changing it to [fit the] Filipino context can be better. ('April', Philippines)

One thing that I could suggest is if you have these kind of different participants culturally, you have to ask them prior to the start of the programme ... what are some practices that they are not allowed to do or to do ... so that things would be cleared up so that others can also understand why it's not done, why it should be done. Like

89

> more ... talking to them or communicating to them ... I guess what we are looking at now is trying to read over the [curriculum] and make it more Filipino ... Filipinos, they have English as their second language ... so we have to make it more Filipino, so that we will be able to understand ... It's not like they are going to translate everything in the [curriculum], but we are going to find a way that Filipino kids or adults or young [people] will be able to understand and then internalise more about the aim and the goal. ('Mirabelle', Philippines)

Another young Filipino person highlighted that the aim was not to do away with the existing curriculum, but rather to work on it to make sure it would be an appropriate fit wherever utilised:

> We will follow the curriculum but we will add more. For example, if our participants are from colleges or universities, we should do research on what appropriate activities are for them ... and then, since we have branches from countries such as in Colombia, then I think that our culture [Philippines] must be involved in the curriculum so that we will have a unique programme ... For example, the mirror activity – maybe we can revise it a little so that the participants will be able to understand ... the things that we want them to learn, and ... they will not be bored. ('Art', Philippines)

In this way, the young people reflected on how the programme began in Colombia, but was created by an American and most global staff were based in the US, which was the best funded of the hubs.

It was clear that the curriculum tended to be seen as particularly American. Some young Americans involved in the programme were also critically aware of how their identity or positionality as Americans might limit their ability to understand or promote peace more broadly:

> I think ... you can't find what we call a 'local peace' without really being able to have that interpersonal connection that allows us to see what others are going through even if we feel like we can't

relate, because they are just so different, and then realising that we actually have something in common that we can get through, and we can work through ... Globally, I have not a clue what 'peace' means ... but to me, I think peace ... at its most basic form is just trying to understand others better than we think we do ... I feel like as an American, in so many ways, I can't answer that question. I just feel like that because of the way that our culture is set up. And this whole ... focus on consumers and this whole 'need what I want, when I want, [to do] what I want to do, when I want to do it' kind of attitude ... I feel like it's really hard to establish then what peace is, how we teach peace, because it's like that focus is so backwards in so many ways. ('Olivia', United States)

While recognising these potential limitations of the 'lens' through which they see the world and peacebuilding, this young woman and others working in the US context typically expressed a commitment to better include and account for their global partners in the programme design, delivery and development. As one young American woman said, when asked for any thoughts on how the programme might improve:

I think ... making the curriculum in our programmes more contextualised for where we're working, looking at more marginalised groups in the developing countries that we're working in, and making this curriculum accessible to them, making it accessible to different groups in the US, including people with physical disabilities, children with special needs ... Right now, we don't have all that nuanced ... customised curriculum to fulfil ... different needs of those groups ... I think that's a huge area in which we can expand and we can grow and really affect more people in the communities in which we work. ('Emily', United States)

Similarly, another young woman in the US elucidated the importance of greater self-reflection on positionality that she had gained through her interactions in the project:

I think it's made me more aware of – especially if I'm going to go into a community – how do I gain respect, how do I not be seen as … an outsider coming in and thinking I have all the answers. You know, I want to be humble in going into a place that's different from where I come from and being really aware of that. ('Emma', United States)

Through these statements, Emma highlights how even a 'local' in the sense of being a fellow national of a particular country will undoubtedly have a number of different experiences and characteristics from those they might work with in a different local community. They thus need to reflect on these to better foster effective peacebuilding practice.

Another of Emma's fellow peer leaders explained how working with global colleagues in the project had helped inform her understandings of conflict and peace more broadly, which could also improve her practice in her own local context:

> Being exposed to ['Sofia' from Colombia] and ['John' from the Philippines] … I've heard their stories, but seeing these people in person and seeing the work that they're doing with [M4P] in relation to specific conflicts and violence that has occurred in their countries … I learned … a lot about what that looks like … how they are adapting [M4P] to meet the needs of their communities. [These are] people that are having much bigger sort of traumatic issues … So, I think that that's been … very eye-opening to learn about different types of conflict, different levels of conflict, looking at conflict on the national level as opposed to any one specific region of DC … knowing, seeing that they used [M4P] in their own languages, the translation across cultures of this … I think that's … a big opportunity … how can we contextualise our curriculum even more to meet the needs of those people? ('Emily', USA)

Can creative approaches transcend boundaries of local/global scales?

In considering these local–global crossovers and peacebuilding, we are interested in whether and how this may occur in and through aesthetic approaches, particularly through the use of dance and creative movement. While we agree with Bleiker that we are beyond the need for legitimising broader engagements with the political, including adopting aesthetic politics in the pursuit of peace,[77] we nevertheless aim to show how such aesthetic politics might have particular relevance in contexts of peacebuilding. Extending the aesthetic framework through deeply exploring dance as an embodied perspective provides a unique angle for interaction and reflection.

As Shank and Schirch explain, when following an elicitive peacebuilding framework, participants work together to create fresh knowledge and take part in critical reflection in which connections are 'made between the local and the global; and people work together for change'.[78] This approach can encompass artistic elements, such as when youth use the power of global hip hop culture to engage in local peacebuilding efforts while offering their messages outward to a wider audience.[79] This aesthetic process of simultaneously speaking and moving in multiple directions can offer a rare lens for further understanding the interrelations of hybridity in both local and global contexts.

In such settings, we may consider the question of 'how political relations travel'.[80] While Suliman focuses on how migrants move and have their movements shaped by politics, we suggest that creative movement is also a vital area for exploration of moving political relations as a physical, relational and conceptual act. We incorporate movement 'into a relational account of the politics of global change, rather than seeing movement as merely a symptom or outcome of such transformations'.[81] In this way, we aim to situate dance politically, including in its prospects for peace.

We remain, however, cognisant that while perhaps inherently political, dance is not inherently peaceful or fair. As Enloe explains, a 'militarizing maneuver can look like a dance, not a struggle, even though the dance might be among unequal partners'.[82] Further limits can arise around the potential commodification of globalising art and prospects for cultural imperialism.[83] Globalisation may function to limit cultural identity and cultural diversity, meanwhile dance carries cultural specificity, and some dances that may be fine in one location could be considered culturally offensive in another context.[84]

Dance can also be instrumentalised for political agendas, including co-option by the State. For example, in writing about the popular dance group Inganzo in Rwanda, Plancke suggests that the group's 'performances seem to be a means for diffusing a political ideology', and that the redesign of their repertoire shores up notions of a Rwandan state that is 'unified and de-ethnicised'.[85] Plancke further proposes that in embodying the idea of a 'New Rwanda', the group's focus on uniformity, may limit individual artistic expression and stoke tensions between ethnic groups.[86] Likewise, in considering dance it is important to avoid homogenising views of local or national contexts when it comes to applying terms like 'local' and 'culture', as aesthetic contestations occur within and between cultures.[87]

Nonetheless, research suggests that dance in conflict-affected areas can be used to engage in practices of anti-hegemony, which can surely contribute to peacebuilding in terms of promoting social justice and inclusion.[88] Just as it is important to consider whether and how dance may be instrumentalised, it is also important to recognise that understandings of the local should be able to account for a range of diverse views within that scale or entity.[89]

Exchanging peace? Hub dances across cultures

To further explore questions of the local–global interface, we engage here in a more detailed discussion of one staple dance activity used in M4P across the case study sites: the hub dance exchange. So, what exactly is a hub dance? The hub dances were short, choreographed movement phrases that were created to 'represent' the local 'hubs' or geographic locations of the programme with the intent of sharing these dances with other hubs and building a network of exchange.

Each hub dance developed differently. For example, they could include four different peer leaders contributing a series of movements drawing on personal and cultural elements, or they could emerge from combining movements developed by students in a previous workshop. The hub dances drew on elements of local dance styles, yet were not formal representations of cultural or historic dances. Rather, they represented what young people were interested in and willing to share in the exchange.

Peer leaders learned the dances from representatives of the other hubs when attending an annual training workshop, where they also received video recordings and descriptive notes for each of the hub dances. Using this knowledge and drawing on these resources, and occasionally utilising live online interaction between programme sites, peer leaders taught the dances to participants across the different sites. Following the creation of a local hub dance, the exchange would likewise include participants learning both their own 'local' hub dance as well as those from other hubs around the world. The process often culminated in an informal public performance. These occurred across a range of settings such as schools, universities, training workshops and community groups.

In some cases, the hub dances prompted a process of co-creation between participants or in response to other hubs. The hub dances, which allow both individual and collective contributions, show how cross-cultural exchange and dialogue may be critical aspects of dance's capacity for supporting peacebuilding. Hub dances can also be used to share stories of one place with another. As some Filipino participants explained:

> In [M4P] we have this so-called hub dance. It's an exchanging of dances from the Philippines, Germany and [other countries] … we also experience understanding our different cultures because our dances or our movements in dancing really varies to our culture, and that helped me understand and appreciate the other culture too. ('Franc', Philippines)
>
> It's the first time for me to see the hub dances of different countries … Hub dance is … expressing different diversity like the culture,

> the music that they use ... I noticed, for example, the Philippines hub dance ... was composed of different culture[s], for example the Muslims, the Christians and the modern Filipino[s]. I'm so very proud that I am part of that, dancing with ... the different hub dances. ('Ben', Philippines)

Similarly, another participant explained how the Filipino dance 'feels Filipino' in a way that embraces heterogeneity at the national level, saying this was

> Because of the different dance steps, like the ethnic steps in Mindanao. Muslims' dance is quite serious ... When the music reached the chorus portion, the emotion changed like you can smile, dance freely and wave your hands, but not to the extent of pushing someone. You have also to give space. ('Jason', Philippines)

Through this physical description of different sections of a hub dance, he alludes to the need for committing to relational approaches that offer space for difference, be it locally, nationally or globally. For 'Jason', the hub dance provided an embodied experience and a metaphorical and literal means for understanding the interaction of different groups in Mindanao. At the same time, he said that the hub dance 'activity was a big challenge' for him, but also exciting.

As these statements highlight, the hub dance practice is meaningful because a significant challenge of peacebuilding is how to 'reconstitute, or restory, the narrative and thereby restore the people's place in history'.[90] Hub dances might also be used to create shared stories. For example, Stock suggests that in some contexts, dancing culturally specific dances of another culture may make for a more culturally inclusive environment.[91] Similarly, Eddy proposes that through appreciating different ways of moving, tolerance of difference may be expanded, and thus: 'Practicing dances from different cultures, when joyful rather than forced, also expands this type of compassion and has been used as a form of conflict resolution internationally.'[92] While Stock argues against dance as a universal language, she nonetheless advocates '*for* the universality of dance in the sense that it is a multisensory representation of the human condition, with common human concerns, emotions, needs and aspirations, albeit expressed in cultural and genre specific ways'.[93]

Of course, more reflection is required when it comes to considerations of how dance, while sometimes described as a universal means for representation, can also be deployed in specific contexts to particular political ends. After all, the programme studied in our research was not often engaging with explicitly political questions, but tended towards a fairly individual focus. In contrast, future initiatives might like to consider concerted efforts to engage participants in developing critical consciousness to support youth to achieve wider peaceful change.

Through their explanations noted above, these young Filipino men suggest both how a simplified view of another country or culture might be transmitted by dance exchange, but also how the local creation of such hub dances can be done in a way that aims to communicate and embrace diversity within the local or national context. It is also worth noting that even well-intentioned efforts to represent diversity in a local or national context could face pitfalls. For example, in the Philippines, this could include the potential for further embedding stereotypes such as the 'modern Filipino' and the 'serious Muslim'. In some cases, individuals with limited dance experience created hub dances, so the steps they drew on became more generalised and arguably less attuned to local experience, even though the choreographers were the local representatives working within the global context.

One young woman from the Philippines suggested that activities like the hub dance require adequate explanation or they may fail to realise the outcomes that programme developers are hoping to achieve:

> The first time that I did the hub dance, I wasn't sure I was doing the right thing ... It would be very important to show the meaning of the dance before doing it because ... I have these questions like

> ... Why would I do this? What is it to me if I'm going to do this? I need to understand so that I can also convey not confusion, but idea or facts to those kids that we are teaching. Though I feel like dancing the dances, [they were] so fun, just doing with the movement ... but the meaning? I don't know. ('Mirabelle', Philippines)

In this way, she highlights potential limitations to understanding dances of 'the other' without adequate explanation. In other words, while recognising the value of dance for communicating across cultural contexts, she also points to the notion that dance is not necessarily a universal language and further modes of communication may need to be engaged to ensure understanding. A young woman from the US echoed a similar sentiment:

> I learned a lot of new things ... how dance exchange is proof of the fact that we all define dance differently, what can be symbolic movement to one person is different in each context. ('Aubrey', USA)

Others noted how, while learning unfamiliar moves could be challenging, it could also be a learning experience. As one young Filipino woman explained:

> First, I was shy imitating the dance moves especially [as] I am not a good dancer or I cannot easily imitate the moves. But I tried and put in my mind that I can do it. It's really fun, great, and you enjoy yourself through that. And you will appreciate and realise that you can do the dance steps of the other countries ... It feels great that you can dance with their moves. ('Jesza', Philippines)

Other participants also noted the value, including fun and knowledge, they felt came from getting to know other countries and cultures through dance. Some of the young Filipino people stated that they felt the hub dances could help contribute to international understanding:

> Hub dances? I like it. ... We had fun in doing the dance. Through that dance, I was able to know the traditional dance steps of the other countries. ('Bea', Philippines)

Local/global dance 'hubs' for peace

> I have learned some of the hub dances reflect their cultures and practices. ('Art', Philippines)

> It's really good that I had experienced hub dances of the other country … practising or doing their culture is not that difficult … There are some people that will discriminate [against] other cultures, but for me, the hub dances are really good. ('April', Philippines)

> It's also fun having different music and steps. With the hub dance, we [were] able to know where the music and steps originated … we got acquainted with the different dance steps and movement from different countries. ('MJ', Philippines)

Similarly, a young woman in the US stated:

> I think I already came to [M4P] with a certain amount of international engagement and awareness and interest. But it has definitely deepened my knowledge of certain parts of the world. ('Makayla', USA)

Overall, these young people felt they had made important connections to youth in other countries and that this could contribute to their shared goal of peacebuilding. Some also noted how the hub dance activity could assist participants in making connections between different aspects of the spectrum of peace and facilitate their abilities to connect with a wider social movement for peace. As one young American woman explained, in terms of programme participants:

> I hope that their experience … awakens them to the fact that they are embedded in a much larger system … their awareness of their own classroom in their school but then the inner cultural nature of [M4P] will awaken in their awareness to communities around the world and connecting them … because they've learned dances from those parts of the world, feeling connected outside of themselves. And I hope that that awareness will make them more engaged in peacebuilding activities. ('Emma', United States)

Others discussed similar points, sharing their belief that M4P could change not only local communities but also the wider world through incremental efforts over the long term. As one articulated:

> In terms of peace at the global level I think that you can very much see … the inklings … of how [M4P] is doing that, and hopefully as the organisation grows … those inklings will get stronger because when you see that students are being able to see these videos from different areas of the world, and they are learning these dances from different areas of the world … when you learn something about other regions … you feel like you have the connection with it … [W]hen you have … a personal connection with something … you want to be friends with that. And, so I feel like that contributes to nonviolence. ('Olivia', United States)

The hub dances thus functioned as a way of building a network of relationships through the exchange of dance. Through her points, Olivia suggests a return to our earlier discussion about scale, both as a concept and, here, as a verb or process: 'scaling' a programme, which was regularly stated to be a key goal of M4P during our research.

Returning to scale: challenges, opportunities and potentially productive tensions

Participants in the research often talked of the concept of scale in the sense of making something available to more people in more places. For the most part, they situated this as an inherently positive thing. As one young woman in the US explained:

> I think that by collaborating and creating a stronger front, I think that's one of our biggest problems in terms of peacebuilding … all of these organisations are doing a great job, but they are their own little islands; they are not working together. I think it's just a matter of time till they start a snowball and come together and create this huge force and movement. It will be something to reckon with. That's my hope. So, it's just a matter of bringing together different

ideas to really make this a prominent thing in our society instead of just like, 'Oh, there is this little organisation that goes to a few schools'. Instead, it would be something that is a full movement that all these organisations are supporting and contributing to. ('Kaylee', United States)

In this way, the idea of 'scaling' the project was valorised to some extent as in and of itself a good thing.

At the same time, young people in the Philippines and Colombia spoke of how connecting to M4P as a global organisation brought weight to their experience in terms of how they might be evaluated should they wish to get involved in other types of peacebuilding or related work in the future:

> I think that my work with [M4P] would help me to [get involved] in other projects because [M4P], has a global reputation. I think that this helps a lot because [it] is a different way [compared to getting] involved in a programme which is only in Colombia … [M4P] is in Germany, in USA, in Philippines. ('Camila', Colombia)

> We have this great honour, for example, that the US [team can] visit Manila. So, I mean if they're [Filipino youth] putting that in their resume, that they've been part of the [M4P] programme, it's innovative. It's been scaled … I believe that it will really help them to get into peacebuilding efforts … Not all people have dance in the curriculum. That's why I am really telling my students [and M4P facilitators] … 'Be happy, congratulations, because … if you go to work with an NGO or go to work for the government, you have this skill you can be proud of. You can put … in your resume that you have the skill and it's amazing.' ('John', Philippines)

Through these descriptions, these M4P peer leaders show how young people in their countries might value, seek out and benefit from global networks in a variety of ways.

At the same time, the young people interviewed for this study pointed to a number of ways that scaling might be limiting or even counterproductive, given that it could conflict with relevant localisation efforts at times. For example, some young men in the Philippines explained:

> If [M4P] wants to really make changes in the Philippines they [should] just focus [on] Mindanao ... and I think making branches – for example, Iligan [is] a two-hour ride. [The peer educators] would probably get exhausted from the long travel period riding a jeep going to Iligan. And, for example, from Tagoloan to Iligan it's two hours and from Tagoloan to Cotabato it's eight hours, so ... I think it's better [to have] ... branches in different regions. It takes some time. ('Franc', Philippines)

> And to improve [M4P], maybe we should have a large group, like having partners in Visayas, in Luzon, so that we will have partners all over the Philippines. It is a part of practising the culture of the Philippines. ('Art', Philippines)

Through these statements, these young Filipinos suggest that at times the local as very narrowly defined may be the most important level to focus on to improve the programme. They were actively engaged in negotiating the interpretation of the local–global exchange in their conceptualisation of the work and, while excited about the international connections, they were also frustrated by the logistical realities on the ground. In short, these dance exchanges occurred in specific spaces, places and times, which shaped the context of participants' performance of the local–global exchange.[94]

Keeping this in mind, perhaps sometimes what is needed is the opposite of scaling – what we might instead conceive of as 'honing', or sharpening the focus to incorporate and respond to contexts that are constantly subject to shifting and contestation. One young American woman explained her view that the programme

> has a lot of potential to create long lasting change ... [as] one programme in a really big world, and we need lots of programmes, and we need lots of current ways to reach lots of people. What works for one person isn't going to work for everyone ... But, I'm

really content with the change that I see [M4P] making in individuals. ('Makayla', United States)

Rather than being content to simply celebrate M4P's success in terms of the number of participants attracted into the programme, she told us:

> I'm more interested in what each individual person is doing differently in their life ... to me that's just as significant. A success is to change one person versus the world, because that one person could go on and change things in the world. So, it has this amplifying power. I think it does have the power to transform the way people think about dance, and the way they think about peace education. It really has a lot of power to get people involved to the extent that it's scalable and people can respond to the programme and they can move it forward into their lives. ('Makayla', United States)

She further clarified that there are limitations or caveats to the utility of scaling:

> I'm really interested in [M4P] maintaining its accessibility to all people who want the programme, and I think any time you scale an idea, there's a danger of heading in a direction where you advertise to people, 'you need this programme because' ... I'm really more interested in [M4P] maintaining an organic feel, being a ... programme that's really as much about people in the communities we are partnering with, as it is about [M4P]. And to that end I think that we need to work on identifying what is culturally relevant in our societies and how can we adapt the curriculum to address certain situations in certain places. Where schools are not the best avenue to reach children, how can we work with out-of-school populations? And it's really thinking through not ... 'Oh, we need X number of partners', or, 'we need to show that we scaled this much in this year', but really making it about the needs of the children and having it be something that's called for in the community ... That's a huge problem in a lot of fields like international engagement [when organisations] replicate ... [this] asymmetry of power that I have been talking about, which is the last thing that I would want

[M4P] to do, but it's hard to find that balance. ('Makayla', United States)

Overall, the young people involved in this study point to the need for thinking about the complexity of scale, including the challenges, opportunities and potential productive tensions that may arise when attempting to connect, translate and look inward as well as outward within and between cultures. Or, as one young woman put it:

> I would love to see [M4P] expand to different nations ... I'd really like to see the curriculum expand and adapt to other communities ... I'm really excited to see ... development of ... movement as a universal language so whether it's using these hub dances to communicate and ... see how that can help to cultivate a global identity as it goes to distinct national identities. ('Samantha', United States)

In short, the work considered here highlights challenges and potentially productive tensions situated where expanding and adapting meet – a task for which dance may be particularly well placed, given its key elements around breath and flexibility.

Conclusion

Throughout this chapter, we have demonstrated that, through looking at young people's practice and understanding of dance and creative movement for peace, we can gain insights around local and global peacebuilding efforts, while also noting how the two are understood, connect and may aid in creating one another. By reflecting on participant statements referring to 'global' and 'local' themes, we have demonstrated how these complex spheres overlap, are not mutually exclusive and do not define the full spectrum of peacebuilding arenas. Nonetheless, because the concept of the local in particular has had such strong resonance both for local communities affected by conflict and for global peace and development actors working alongside them, we believe further investigating the local and the global has been an important endeavour.

By listening to the young people involved in this study across the three case study sites, we learned about how they contest their marginalisation from formal political efforts at building peace. Instead of accepting this, the young people we worked with explained how they envision peace, like violence, as occurring on a spectrum that crosses a number of scales or spheres. Many of them saw this as beginning with the self or the individual and connecting out to the local community, as well as more broadly working to create global communities committed to peace. For young people, in particular, this offered important connections they could use both in building peace and in building opportunities for themselves in a globally connected world that values international networks.

The participants said that they found dance a particularly relevant way for making these global connections for peace, given that, while dance may not be a universal language, it is nonetheless commonly understood as a platform for sharing meaning, including across difference. At the same time, many of them felt more work needed to be done to 'translate' the programme across cultures to ensure local relevance and respect for various cultural contexts. Incorporating this feedback into future programmes could mean efforts at 'honing' the programme at times through reflecting on, adjusting and deepening the relationships between local and global participants and hubs rather than focusing uncritically on 'scaling'.

In addition to engaging with participants' general statements regarding local–global interactions more broadly, we have also taken a detailed look at micro-level local–global exchange efforts by considering how participants created and shared hub dances – group dance exchange activities – across and between programme sites. In doing so, we interrogated the political implications of this interchange and/or co-creation. According to the interviewees, these opportunities for cross-cultural exchange provided opportunities to (re)articulate, explain and share their own identities while also connecting with and better understanding different cultural contexts affected by conflict. To consider how this might support peacebuilding, we explored tensions between prospects and challenges, including whether dance ideas might be homogenised in ways that foster stereotypes, and/or how individual or group identities might be presented or understood in ways that make space for valuing difference. While the outcomes are complex, we suggest that through creating, practising and exchanging such cross-cultural dance offerings, activities like the hub dances may foster the (re)creation of meaning for self, others and communities, and when done reflectively, this may play a role in contributing to broader efforts to build a culture of peace in plural contexts.

Notes

1 J. P. Lederach, *The Moral Imagination: The Art and Soul of Building Peace* (Oxford: Oxford University Press, 2005), p. 56.
2 L. J. Pruitt, 'Global youth and peacebuilding', in *Handbook of Peace and Conflict Studies*, ed. by S. Byrne, T. Matyok and I. Scott (New York: Routledge, 2019), p. 327.
3 M. Sukarieh and S. Tannock, *Youth Rising? The Politics of Youth in the Global Economy* (New York and London: Routledge, 2015), p. 2.
4 Pruitt, 'Global youth and peacebuilding'.
5 L. B. Wilcox, *Bodies of Violence: Theorizing Embodied Subjects in International Relations* (Oxford: Oxford University Press, 2015).
6 S. Marston, 'The social construction of scale', *Progress in Human Geography*, 24 (2000), p. 232.
7 *Ibid.*, p. 220; A. Björkdahl and S. Buckley-Zistel, *Spatializing Peace and Conflict: Mapping the Production of Places, Sites and Scales of Violence* (London: Palgrave Macmillan, 2016), p. 5.
8 Marston, 'The social construction of scale', p. 220; E. Swyngedouw, 'Neither global nor local: glocalization and the politics of scale', in *Spaces of Globalization: Reasserting the Power of the Local*, ed. by K. Cox (New York: Guilford, 1997), p. 142.
9 N. Smith, 'Contours of a spatialized politics: homeless vehicles and the production of geographical scale', *Social Text*, 33 (1992), p. 73.
10 Marston, 'The social construction of scale'; Smith, 'Contours of a spatialized politics'.

11 Marston, 'The social construction of scale', p. 219.
12 Swyngedouw, 'Neither global nor local', p. 140.
13 Björkdahl and Buckley-Zistel, *Spatializing Peace and Conflict*; Marston, 'The social construction of scale'; Swyngedouw, 'Neither global nor local'.
14 D. Delaney and H. Leitner, 'The political construction of scale', *Political Geography*, 16 (1997), pp. 94–5; Swyngedouw, 'Neither global nor local', p. 140.
15 Marston, 'The social construction of scale'.
16 S. Buckley-Zistel, 'Frictional spaces: transitional justice between the global and the local', in *Friction and Peacebuilding: Global and Local Encounters in Post-Conflict Societies*, ed. by A. Björkdahl *et al*. (Abingdon: Routledge, 2016), p. 25; Swyngedouw, 'Neither global nor local', pp. 137–9.
17 S. Kappler, *Local Agency and Peacebuilding* (Basingstoke: Palgrave Macmillan, 2014), p. 22.
18 Björkdahl and Buckley-Zistel, *Spatializing Peace and Conflict*, p. 2; Swyngedouw, 'Neither global nor local'.
19 Swyngedouw, 'Neither global nor local', pp. 140–2.
20 F. Anderl, 'The myth of the local: how international organizations localize norms rhetorically', *Review of International Organizations*, 11 (2016), p. 200.
21 Buckley-Zistel, 'Frictional spaces', p. 26.
22 H. Johnson, 'Narrating entanglements: rethinking the local/global divide in ethnographic migration research', *International Political Sociology*, 10 (2016), pp. 383–97.
23 Anderl, 'The myth of the local', p. 198; T. Paffenholz, 'Unpacking the local turn in peacebuilding: a critical assessment towards an agenda for future research', *Third World Quarterly*, 36 (2015), pp. 857–74.
24 A. Brown *et al*., 'Challenging statebuilding as peacebuilding: working with hybrid political orders to build peace', in *Palgrave Advances in Peacebuilding: Critical Developments and Approaches*, ed. by O. P. Richmond (Basingstoke: Palgrave Macmillan, 2010), pp. 99–115.
25 Anderl, 'The myth of the local', p. 198.
26 *Ibid*., p. 215.
27 R. Mac Ginty, 'Where is the local? Critical localism and peacebuilding', *Third World Quarterly*, 36 (2015), p. 840.
28 Anderl, 'The myth of the local', p. 212.
29 A. Henrizi, 'Building peace in hybrid spaces: women's agency in Iraqi NGOs', *Peacebuilding*, 3 (2015), p. 88.
30 Anderl, 'The myth of the local', p. 199.
31 K. R. Cox, 'Spaces of dependence, spaces of engagement and the politics of scale, or: looking for local politics', *Political Geography*, 17 (1998), pp. 1–24.
32 M. Brown, 'Sex, scale and the "new urban politics": HIV-prevention strategies from Yaletown, Vancouver', in *Mapping Desire: Geographies of*

Sexualities, ed. by D. Bell and G. Valentine (London and New York: Routledge, 1995), pp. 245–63.
33 L. Staeheli, 'Empowering political struggle: spaces and scales of resistance', *Political Geography Compass*, 13 (1994), p. 388.
34 Anderl, 'The myth of the local', p. 217; B. Bräuchler and P. Naucke, 'Peacebuilding and conceptualisations of the local', *Social Anthropology*, 25 (2017), pp. 422–36.
35 R. Paris, 'Peacebuilding and the limits of liberal internationalism', *International Security*, 22 (1997), p. 56.
36 T. Bierschenk, 'From the anthropology of development to the anthropology of global social engineering', *Zeitschrift für Ethnologie*, 139 (2014), p. 76.
37 B. Bräuchler, 'Social engineering the local for peace', *Social Anthropology*, 25 (2017), p. 439.
38 Paris, 'Peacebuilding and the limits of liberal internationalism'.
39 See e.g. R. Mac Ginty and O. P. Richmond, 'The local turn in peace building: a critical agenda for peace', *Third World Quarterly*, 43 (2013), pp. 763–83.
40 J. P. Lederach, *Building Peace: Sustainable Reconciliation in Divided Societies* (Washington DC: United States Institute of Peace, 1997); K. Avruch, *Culture and Conflict Resolution* (Washington DC: United States Institute of Peace Press, 1998); B. Bräuchler, 'The cultural turn in peace research: prospects and challenges', *Peacebuilding*, 6 (2018), p. 20.
41 Mac Ginty and Richmond, 'The local turn in peace building'.
42 Bräuchler, 'Social engineering the local for peace', p. 440.
43 C. MacLeod, 'Conclusion: new choreographies of conflict', in *The Choreography of Resolution*, ed. by M. LeBaron, C. MacLeod and A. F. Acland (Chicago: American Bar Association, Section of Dispute Resolution, 2013), p. 554.
44 M. B. Anderson and L. Olson, *Confronting War: Critical Lessons for Peace Practitioners* (Cambridge, MA: The Collaborative for Development Action, 2003), p. 32.
45 Bräuchler, 'Social engineering the local for peace', p. 440.
46 Buckley-Zistel, 'Frictional spaces', p. 21.
47 C. Pedwell, 'Affective (self-) transformations: empathy, neoliberalism and international development', *Feminist Theory*, 13 (2012), p. 175.
48 V. Boege, P. Rinck, and T. Debiel, 'Local–international relations and the recalibration of peacebuilding interventions: insights from the "laboratory" of Bougainville and beyond', INEF report (Duisburg: Institute for Development and Peace, University of Duisburg-Essen, 2017), p. 42.
49 Bräuchler, 'Social engineering the local for peace', p. 448.
50 Bräuchler, 'The cultural turn in peace research', p. 17.

Local/global dance 'hubs' for peace

51 O. P. Richmond, 'A genealogy of peace and conflict theory', in *Palgrave Advances in Peacebuilding: Critical Developments and Approaches*, ed. by O. P. Richmond (Basingstoke: Palgrave Macmillan, 2010), p. 33.
52 Bräuchler, 'The cultural turn in peace research', p. 17.
53 *Ibid.*, p. 5.
54 Bräuchler, 'Social engineering the local for peace', p. 440.
55 Bräuchler, 'The cultural turn in peace research', p. 20.
56 *Ibid.*, p. 6.
57 *Ibid.*, pp. 1–2.
58 Bräuchler, 'Social engineering the local for peace'.
59 *Ibid.*, p. 446; Avruch, *Culture and Conflict* Resolution, pp. 20–1.
60 Bräuchler, 'The cultural turn in peace research', p. 18.
61 Bräuchler, 'Social engineering the local for peace', p. 449; Bräuchler and Naucke, 'Peacebuilding and conceptualisations of the local'.
62 Bräuchler, 'Social engineering the local for peace', p. 439.
63 S. Benhabib, *The Claims of Culture: Equality and Diversity in the Global Era* (Princeton: Princeton University Press, 2002).
64 A. Harris, *Young People and Everyday Multiculturalism* (New York and London: Routledge, 2013), p. 141; (quote p. 33).
65 S. McEvoy-Levy, 'Children, youth and peacebuilding', in *Critical Issues in Peace and Conflict Studies: Theory, Practice and Pedagogy*, ed. by T. Matyok, J. Senehi and S. Byrne (Lanham: Lexington Books, 2011), p. 159.
66 *Ibid.*, p. 169.
67 *Ibid.*
68 *Ibid.*
69 *Ibid.*, p. 161.
70 *Ibid.*
71 *Ibid.*
72 S. L. Foster, 'Choreographies of protest', *Theatre Journal*, 55 (2003), p. 397.
73 McEvoy-Levy, 'Children, youth and peacebuilding', p. 169.
74 *Ibid.*, p. 170.
75 *Ibid.*, p. 163.
76 S. Engle Merry, *Human Rights and Gender Violence: Translating International Law into Local Justice* (Chicago: University of Chicago Press, 2006); N. Bubant, 'Vernacular security: the politics of feeling safe in global, national and local worlds', *Security Dialogue*, 36 (2005), pp. 275–96.
77 R. Bleiker, 'In search of thinking space: reflections on the aesthetic turn in international political theory', *Millennium: Journal of International Studies*, 45 (2017), pp. 258–64.
78 M. Shank and L. Schirch, 'Strategic arts-based peacebuilding', *Peace and Change*, 33 (2008), p. 223.
79 *Ibid.*

80 S. Suliman, 'Mobility and the kinetic politics of migration and development', *Review of International Studies*, 42 (2016), p. 20.
81 *Ibid.*, p. 21.
82 C. Enloe, *Maneuvers: The International Politics of Militarizing Women's Lives* (Berkeley: University of California Press, 2000), p. 10.
83 P. D. Facci, 'On human potential: peace and conflict transformation fostered through dance' (Master's dissertation, Universitat Innsbruck, 2011), p. 115.
84 C. Stock, 'Myth of a universal dance language: tensions between globalisation and cultural difference', in *Asia Pacific Dance Bridge: Academic Conference, Papers and Abstracts*, ed. by S. Burridge (Singapore: World Dance Alliance, 2001), pp. 246–62.
85 C. Plancke, 'Dance performances in post-genocide Rwanda: remaking identity, reconnecting present and past', *Journal of Eastern African Studies*, 11 (2017), p. 339.
86 *Ibid.*, pp. 339–40.
87 N. Rowe, 'Dance education in the Occupied Palestinian Territories: hegemony, counter-hegemony and anti-hegemony', *Research in Dance Education*, 9 (2008), pp. 3–20; N. Rowe, 'Movement politics: dance criticism in the Occupied Palestinian Territories', *Forum for Modern Language Studies*, 46 (2010), pp. 441–59; H. Neveu Kringelbach, 'Moving shadows of Casamance: performance and regionalism in Senegal', in *Dancing Cultures: Globalization, Tourism and Identity in the Anthropology of Dance*, ed. by H. Neveu Kringelbach and J. Skinner (New York and Oxford: Berghahn Books, 2012), pp. 143–60.
88 N. Rowe, 'Dance and political credibility: the appropriation of Dabkeh by Zionism, Pan-Arabism, and Palestinian Nationalism', *Middle East Journal*, 65 (2011), pp. 363–80.
89 Lederach, *The Moral Imagination*, p. 146.
90 *Ibid.*
91 Stock, 'Myth of a universal dance language'.
92 M. Eddy, 'Dancing solutions to conflict: field-tested somatic dance for peace', *Journal of Dance Education*, 16 (2016), p. 107.
93 Stock, 'Myth of a universal dance language', p. 253.
94 S. M. Rai, 'Political performance: a framework for analysing democratic politics', *Political Studies*, 63 (2014), pp. 1179–97.

4
Finding empathy and practising peace through dance: through a mirror darkly?

> *The whole concept is kind of for the empathy. It's like movement-based learning … I can identify my emotions better when they're expressed through movement than when they're just cold to me.*
>
> 'Claire', M4P founder, United States

Imagine a crowded university classroom in Mindanao, on the edge of the active conflict region in the Philippines. The room is filled with dancing, moving students who are focused on each other with a heightened energy. Many students are meeting for the first time, in some cases coming from communities that are in conflict with each other. In this scene, the eye focuses on four people in the centre of the room. In the foreground, there is a pair made up of a young man and a young woman, their outstretched arms glimpsed in a blur of movement.

Even though they had not interacted before this exercise, there is a close attentiveness and intent in their pose, accompanied by a slight sense of mischief. The young woman is the leader and she does not seem intimidated by the fact that she is partnered with one of the programme facilitators. Surrounding them are thirty-five additional pairs of students, all working simultaneously. Despite the very close quarters, everyone manages to navigate the space together. They are all engaged in a mirroring activity, intently focused and emotionally connected to their partners, even if just for a few minutes.

Attending to emotions is a key element of building positive peace. In particular, creating and developing empathy has been identified as one crucial aspect of this emotional dimension of peacebuilding. Through simultaneously engaging with the established literature and our own research data, we deepen the exploration of the role of emotions and empathy in peacebuilding. As researchers have established, empathy is essential for restructuring relationships after violence. Likewise, we consider links between empathy and mirroring.

Mirroring is a well-established dance activity that is used in many settings and contexts, including theatre, dance therapy, dance education and community dance. This chapter explores the concept of practising peace by critically reflecting on activities that incorporate the use of mirroring. As seen in our three case studies, peace must be practised, and the process of mirroring provides opportunities for this by inviting interpersonal exchange and the building of empathy. These, in turn, establish safe venues and structures through which to see, understand and feel the presence of others across difference. Of course, empathy in general and mirroring in particular can also have their challenges or limits, which we also explore.

This chapter makes a few key points: (a) nonviolent engagement with, and expression of, emotions are vital to peacebuilding; (b) empathy can play an important role in emotional peacebuilding; and finally, (c) dance and creative movement activities, such as the use of mirroring, when done reflectively, can be valuable practices for developing empathy and supporting peacebuilding.

Emotions, dance and the politics of building peace

Emotions permeate international politics from elite levels to grassroots activism and calls for revolutionary change.[1] Moreover: 'Emotions are woven through the causes and experiences of violent conflict. Yet they remain sidelined by politicians, negotiators, governments, armed forces and international institutions.'[2] Furthermore, although world politics has traditionally been perceived as rational interactions sitting outside the emotional realm, political decision-making cannot be devoid of emotions, since they 'exist at the core of human life'.[3] Excluding emotions likewise has political consequences for a range of actors, as exclusions of 'different ways of knowing beyond traditional rationalist/positivist frameworks … have functioned historically to exclude or devalue marginalised people's knowledge'.[4] This extends to considering pluralism and attention to nonverbal expression, since looking beyond verbal approaches can improve our understanding of the political and enable us to better see the pluralism underpinning the human experience.[5]

Emotions here 'are interpreted most productively not as affective lenses on "truth" or "reality", but rather as one important (embodied) circuit through which power is felt, imagined, mediated, negotiated and/or contested'.[6] A variety of emotions – such as anger, pride, dignity, disrespect, humiliation, love and sadness – are encountered often in conflict and in reconciliation, as well as in dance. Moreover, emotions are clearly vital to peacebuilding, since emotions play important roles in times of trauma, not least because emotions play political roles in how communities recover and/or endure.[7]

This politics of emotion is certainly relevant to the study of dance and peacebuilding. After all, as political theorist Chantal Mouffe suggests, the great power of art rests 'in its capacity to make us see things in a different way, to make us perceive new possibilities', and dance provides a unique way of doing so.[8] This is essential for peacebuilding, because changing the way people see themselves and others is a critical aspect of transforming conflict, and emotions are an essential part of this ongoing process.[9]

After all, motion and emotion are connected, and dancers must learn to be responsible for their own feelings and to manage them in relation to the dance and their dance partner.[10] Moreover, for some, group dancing is seen to be 'the great leveler and binder of human communities, uniting all who participate'.[11] Ehrenreich, referring to the cathartic aspects of dancing in settings such as concerts or carnivals, even went so far as to say: 'In synchronous movement to music or chanting voices, the petty rivalries and factional differences that might divide a group could be transmuted into harmless competition over one's prowess as a dancer, or forgotten.'[12] Mouffe similarly suggests that artistic practices can foster new forms of subjectivity, since through engaging emotions they can connect to people 'at the affective level'.[13] Grau articulates dance as being powerful because it brings together intellect, reason and cognition with affect, emotion and feeling through acts of embodied relationality.[14] In other words, it is precisely because artistic practices like dance and creative movement call upon emotion that they have the capacity to help people (re)create themselves and others in the pursuit of peace.

Recognising the importance of emotions to address conflict and build peace further necessitates thinking about and with bodies. After all, physical sensation is both a source and an expression of emotions.[15] Our physical states and our emotions are related, and both can move and shift, even during conflict. This evokes curiosity around what dance and creative movement might have to offer when it comes to peacebuilding, which requires emotional, conceptual and interpersonal shifts – all of which can flow from physical movement or be restricted by the lack of movement.[16]

Likewise, transformative approaches to conflict, including a number of aspects embodied in dance – such as relationality, imagination, flexibility, curiosity, creativity, rhythm, bodily tacit knowledge and emotionality – have been encouraged in literature on second-generation negotiation.[17] The tactics of movement and breath control can be deployed to foster flexibility instead of rigidity in the face of strong emotions. In other words, peacebuilding requires us to become open to the unfamiliar, and dance's physical nature

Finding empathy, practising peace through dance

can assist with this: 'It jolts our perceptions, physically shakes us up, and, as important, because when we dance we resonate with others physically and emotionally, it creates new bridges of connection.'[18]

As one young woman in the Philippines explained, the lack of capacity to express emotions in constructive ways can be associated with, or limited by, the occurrence of violence:

> If there is violence in the community, people will not be able to communicate well because there's always this outrage of emotions and some of the people will get so scared and not participate any more. ('Mirabelle', Philippines)

The ability to address, express and respond to emotions in nonviolent ways was a key theme for the participants in terms of how they saw dance as relevant for peacebuilding. When asked whether and how dance had been useful for their involvement in peacebuilding, many interviewees pointed to its links with emotion. For example, when asked whether they felt dance and/or movement had been a useful tool for their involvement in peacebuilding, Colombian participants responded as follows:

> Yes, dance is a tool that allows expressing emotions and feelings. I think that is very important because I've always believed that almost everything begins with expression; expression of what I feel and what I live internally. If I don't express or transmit that energy, it will go against others. ('Alejandro', Colombia)

> Yes, totally. I believe that with dance and with the body you can express many things and many feelings you have inside, whether they are feelings of happiness, joy or sadness. ('Valeria', Colombia)

> Yes, it has been very useful because it has helped me become more sensitive … about my feelings in certain situations and how I could project those feelings in another person and how they could feel in certain situations. ('Ximena', Colombia)

Dancing through the dissonance

Similarly, participants in the Philippines expressed:

> I'm starting to internalise how movement can really affect your personality and then transferring your real emotion inside with movement to others, conveying your message to them through your movement ... Incorporating it is such a good thing. ('Mirabelle', Philippines)

> By dancing we can express our emotions. For example, if we are happy, we keep on jumping. If we are sad, we can still make ourselves happy by listening to upbeat music. ('Jason', Philippines)

> When you look at a person dancing, I can see peace in them. I can see that they are happy because they are dancing. The way they move in dancing [is] like expressing their feelings. There I can see peace in them ... You can see peace in dancing if you do it with emotion, showing or expressing ... your true feelings inside. ('MJ', Philippines)

'MJ' also noted that his involvement in the M4P programme had taught him skills around emotional management that would help him address future conflict nonviolently: 'I learned that there are many ways to control your temper ... managing emotions. Because people nowadays easily get angry.'

A number of M4P peer leaders in the US also referred to their sense that emotions and their relation to connection and understanding could be important in peacebuilding. One young woman explained that she felt the M4P programmes would assist participants with getting involved in other peacebuilding work in the future, and she directly linked this to its emotional elements:

> I think having this ... platform to learn about the basics of peacebuilding, to learn ... even more sort of foundational building blocks and what is needed for peace, so understanding that handling a conflict by using empathy rather than violence ... that's Step 1 ... learning strategies to handle their emotions as opposed to acting out or finding another outlet that might not be healthy ... I think that

Finding empathy, practising peace through dance

these foundational building blocks are really crucial in understanding what peacebuilding is and having that … as part of their personal experience, I think it's huge if they ever do want to get involved in peacebuilding because it's a great experience for them to use and to leverage. ('Emily', United States)

While in broad agreement, another young woman in the US noted the caveat that of course these programmes cannot address all issues in some kind of silo and must be part of a longer-term process of engaging individuals and communities in nonviolence:

I do believe that social and emotional learning programmes can decrease violence. I think it's more difficult when you start with older children. I think it really has to start young. You have to build a culture that is nonviolent and it's hard work, so I think that we are part of a larger picture … When kids are toddlers, are you punishing them with violence, are you letting it be okay when they act violently? It starts very, very young. ('Emma', United States)

While some scholars have demonstrated an interest in connections between emotions, arts and peacebuilding,[19] as well as around collective emotions and peacebuilding, including links with artistic practices in theatre,[20] further exploration in this area is needed, particularly in relation to dance. After all, Beausoleil has identified empathy as a 'major intersection between dance and conflict'.[21] With research suggesting that empathy can be learned,[22] dance and creative movement emerge as a viable means for facilitating such peace education. According to Alexander and LeBaron, these embodied practices can be effective in conflict-affected settings because 'they can quickly and deeply foster intergroup trust, receptivity and flexibility when encountering the unfamiliar'.[23] Despite this support in the research, and although recognition has grown around the need to address the emotional dimensions of conflict and empathy's prime position in the 'transformative toolbox, it has been given little explicit critical attention'.[24] The next section addresses this by focusing on empathy, a key factor for consideration in relation to conflict, emotions and peacebuilding through dance.

Explaining empathy

Empathy is an interdisciplinary, messy and complex concern. Competing definitions abound, though some commonalities tend to emerge. According to Swick: 'Empathy is a process where a person senses how others feel about their situation and is able to then respond to the situation in a caring way.'[25] Similarly, Sams and Truscott state that, 'empathy refers to the various ways in which people experience and respond to others' affective or psychological states'.[26] Jolliffe and Farrington note that definitions of empathy have described it 'as an affective trait which facilitates the experience of the emotions of another person', 'a cognitive ability which facilitates the understanding of the emotions of another person' and a combination of the two.[27] Meanwhile, Stephan and Finlay suggest that theorists and researchers tend to agree that two essential types of empathy exist: cognitive and emotional. While a variety of terms are used for each of the types, cognitive empathy mostly refers to taking another person's perspective, while emotional empathy mostly refers 'to emotional responses to another person that either are similar to those the other person is experiencing (parallel empathy) or are a reaction to the emotional experiences of the other person (reactive empathy)'.[28]

Noting that definitions of empathy differ across a range of literatures, Pedwell suggests that it is typically understood as akin 'to other "humanizing" emotions such as sympathy and compassion in denoting an orientation of care or concern towards others', while also being distinct 'on the basis of the stronger element of identification or "perspective taking"'.[29] Similarly, Head suggests: 'Empathy is generally accepted as a mode of being which connects us to others and which promotes intersubjective relations, enabling the individual subject to move beyond the limits of her own

Finding empathy, practising peace through dance

knowledge.'[30] In short, as Head explains: 'Empathy is a term that has been widely adopted in different literatures and for which there is no single, coherent, and consistent meaning, although broad similarities can be traced across definitions and uses.'[31]

For our part, where a definition is required, we adopt Head's explanation of empathy 'as an intersubjective, dynamic, cognitive, and emotional process that operates across multiple timescales. It involves a cognitive understanding of the other's point of view as well as, potentially, the sharing of emotions.'[32] We also note and affirm her premise that, while empathy is integral to political and social life, it is undertheorised when it comes to IR.[33] Empathy also has a physical dimension, which will be addressed later in this chapter. In attempting to understand empathy in peacebuilding efforts, a broader, interdisciplinary lens is required.

Empathy as essential for peacebuilding

Empathy is ripe for further investigation in relation to peacebuilding. Whether or not it is defined, or regardless of the definition chosen in any given context, empathy has been understood as a core aspect linked to peacebuilding.[34] This link has even been situated among key assumptions most peacebuilders share.[35]

In particular, as Head suggests, empathy holds potential for transforming the self and relationships with others, including through creating cognitive dissonance, which she argues can serve as 'a constructive vehicle for social and political transformation'.[36] This sense of cognitive dissonance is not always comfortable and is important to keep in mind in understanding the complexities of empathy. Moreover, empathy may also emerge as a local practice that marginalised people living under occupation engage in 'as part of a strategy of resistance' with emancipatory potential in 'its creative focus on what it is to be human under occupation'.[37] Finally, Head suggests this has important repercussions when analysing empathy through a political lens: 'Viewing empathy as a form of resistance unsettles the traditional categories of "empathiser" (stronger) and "sufferer" (weaker party).'[38]

The capacity for empathy to affect the likelihood of engagement in violence or prospects for peacebuilding appears related to its link with understanding and responding to our own emotions and those of others. As Swick explains: 'To be empathic is to be able to read the cues received from others regarding their feelings', which we may recognise through 'nonverbal gestures, facial expressions, body positioning, tone of voice, and other nonverbal actions'.[39] The nuance of customary and cultural understanding in nonverbal communication is also important to take into consideration. Likewise, empathy incorporates awareness of the self and others, given that recognising and expressing one's own feelings is requisite for understanding others.[40] Research also suggests that self-esteem supports the development of empathy, while, conversely, a lack of empathy tends to relate to behaviours like self-harm.[41]

Empathy has been strongly linked to preventing, reducing or transforming violence. For example, extensive research with children has shown 'a negative relationship between empathy and aggression'.[42] Likewise, scholars of early childhood education have proposed that empathy is necessary for violence prevention and that a lack of empathy can enable violence.[43] While not always able to demonstrate causal order, a number of studies have also associated low empathy with bullying, such as Jolliffe and Farrington's study, which reported that 'for both males and females only a comparably small number took part in frequent bullying and it is these who had low empathy'.[44]

Researchers studying youth have also posited a negative relationship between empathy and violence. Sams and Truscott, for example, found that high exposure to community violence along with low empathy were significant predictors for violent behaviour; likewise, based on their research and related studies, they suggest that 'low empathy may serve as a risk factor to future violent behavior'.[45] This may be especially important in settings with high levels of community violence, such as in many parts of the US, where the vast majority of youth in urban contexts 'have witnessed violent acts including shootings, stabbings, beatings, homicides and thefts'.[46]

Empathy, however, is significant for peacebuilding beyond claims of direct violence-prevention efforts. Empathy can be understood as essential to positive peace, or peace with justice. Empathy has been theorised as necessary for cooperation.[47] Moreover, empathy has been theorised as counter to hierarchy and thus conceptualised as enabling the possibility of transformation.[48] It has also been considered an intrinsic value necessary to promote a kinder world in the political and policy environment.[49] Empathy also strongly relates to leadership development, including around addressing injustices.[50]

Moreover, research suggests that empathy can play a role 'in improving intergroup relations', including through reducing prejudice, understood as negative attitudes toward social groups'.[51] Noting that lack of empathy can negatively affect behaviours and attitudes, research suggests that the presence of empathy can conversely have a range of positive impacts on attitudes and behaviour, and that these changes may persist over time.[52]

Participants in our study explicitly mentioned empathy as an important aspect of how dance could support peacebuilding through facilitating access to emotional dimensions, especially in relation to empathy. As one young woman in the US articulated:

> I think that this progression with [M4P] makes lot of sense about getting into your emotions and how they affect your behaviour and then building that empathy for other people and developing various strategies to help with conflict resolution and peacebuilding. ('Kaylee', United States)

Another young woman described the role of vulnerability and trust and how these elements contribute to valuing diverse perspectives. She explained how she believed the programme could reduce violent events in the community because it could assist in building empathy between people and using movement to build trust. In her opinion, this possibility arose from the vulnerability embodied in dancing together. In doing so, she says, 'you start to build a trusting relationship'. ('Samantha', United States)

Similarly, a young male facilitator in the Philippines explained:

> This work [dance and creative movement for peace] creates an emotion ... Different emotions are expressed by the participants depending also on the topics like being sad or talking about bullying. Empathy must transpire among the participants because that's what we want to them to know and learn. ('Art', Philippines)

This same young man expressed how he had experienced this empathy development himself as part of working with the project. In terms of relating to others, he said:

> I empathise with them. Before, I was really shy, I can't communicate well with others, I don't talk too much. Yes, I see myself with other people and with that I was able to understand them. ('Art', Philippines)

Many participants reported that they felt empathy was a skill they had developed through their participation in M4P:

> I think the biggest skill that I have acquired is empathy, is putting myself in the place of others ... now I think I can handle my conflicts a little better, because now I think of others instead of thinking only of myself. ('Valeria', Colombia)

> The first thing is ... having in mind what I'm doing and ... time to think about things and not to take actions that I can later possibly regret. And as a result [of] that come other things, like empathy and respect with and for others, to accept and not fight for those differences. ('Luciana', Colombia)

> I think that [with] empathy, I learned how to recognise the necessity of living in a community and respecting the other's opinions, to value them, have them in mind and listen and observe. ('Ximena', Colombia)

Finding empathy, practising peace through dance

A young Filipino man likewise explained how he felt this capacity to develop empathy was a core way in which M4P could change the community:

> [M4P] is promoting anti-bullying activities. Just imagine if young kids had developed empathy [they wouldn't] hurt other kids because they [would] know what the other kids would feel if they [did] something bad [to] the other kids. And so, because of that we can build a very, very harmonious and better community. ('Franc', Philippines)

Another young Filipino man explained that he would start

> encouraging my friends to be part of this because if you are going to undergo this training it will be a good change with their lives. For example, with their attitude, it will develop one's self-confidence, empathy, [and it] stops bullying. ('Ben', Philippines)

If considering emotions in general and empathy in particular as relating most directly to how one sees or understands others, several further links arise in participants' accounts of their experiences in dance and creative movement for peacebuilding. For example, a number of young people reported that participating in this dance-based peacebuilding programme had helped break down stereotypes that they previously held. In the Philippines, much of this seemed to relate to the programme facilitating their interactions with young people from backgrounds different to their own, especially when it came to religion, but also across other factors of difference, such as indigenous identity:

> When I was young, when they talk[ed] about Moros or the Muslims, we were thinking that they are bad guys, and, if they know that I am Christian, they would probably kill me or kick out my head and do something bad. But then when I joined [M4P], I got the chance to meet different people: Muslims, natives, some of them don't have religion … but I had to respect them because that is their belief and that is their own culture. Yeah, it has changed me a lot … I think out of 100 only 10 per cent, only 10 people know that we need

> to respect Muslims. I mean, they are just like us. I mean, there is bad Catholic, there is good Catholic, and there is also good and bad Muslim. It's not the religion that matters, it's not the belief, it's not the culture. ('Franc', Philippines)

> I have a classmate who is a Lumad ... Before I thought that the [Lumad] are different and we should not mingle with them because they have different perception[s], especially with their cultures and traditions. But now I understand that we should give them respect with regard to their culture or traditions so that they will also respect our culture. ('Jesza', Philippines)

While not as commonly as with the Filipinos, Colombian participants also reported changed views of others:

> Well, mostly it has changed the way I look at others. Sometimes you judge without knowing or sometimes react to people without putting yourself in their shoes. Implementing the project with children in vulnerable populations such as Ciudad Bolivar, I realised it's not that they do not want to do things, but that they may have feelings that don't let them, or that maybe they just left their house after being beaten. So, what I feel has changed me the most is the power to put myself in the place of others before judging them, and that there are many ways to manage conflict, that aggression is not necessary to solve problems. ('Valeria', Colombia)

A politics of empathy

Empathy may also stir social action in pursuit of justice. As Stephan and Finlay note, cognitive empathy can reduce prejudice and discrimination through enabling people to see commonalities with other groups.[53] On the whole, empathy can be a favourable tool for improving intergroup relations;[54] and where 'parallel empathy creates a sense of injustice on behalf of the outgroup members', members of in-groups may even 'be stirred to social action'.[55]

Feminist and anti-racist theories have posited that empathy is critical for realising social justice at the global level.[56] Such scholars argue that through empathy, assumptions and hierarchies around factors such as class, race and gender can be challenged, and thus empathy 'may function to promote more ethical relations between people as well as meaningful action and change across cultural and social divides'.[57] At the same time, other critical scholars have suggested the crucial 'need to locate empathy within its sociopolitical context and recognise the asymmetries of power embedded in relationships'.[58]

Likewise, while Pedwell cautions that the transnational politics of empathy require critical reflection, including attention to postcolonial legacies and structural adjustment, she also considers this domain an area with potential for supporting transformative social change.[59] This can transpire, she argues, if, where relevant, a transnational politics of empathy allows those engaged in efforts at building empathy 'to recognise their own complicity within transnational hierarchies of power' so that it becomes possible to create the grounds for social action to interrogate 'structural relations of power that uphold gendered, classed and racialised inequalities transnationally'.[60]

Numerous scholars have suggested limits or challenges in relation to empathy, so a critical political analysis is necessary to delineate clearly whether and how efforts that foster empathy might also facilitate the pursuit of peace. Head suggests that mainstream discourses around empathy typically assume 'a normative, progressive dimension' without accounting for the political dimensions, since much of the existing debate on the subject fails to effectively analyse 'the sociopolitical conditions in which empathy may or may not operate' and does not 'recognise the political character of empathy when it is adopted by actors'.[61] Further, it is important to be cautious of assumptions that experiencing empathy will inherently immediately lead to action, a moral life, change or new decision-making.[62] Indeed, reflections from our research participants in the Philippines included a sense of frustration at experiencing empathy and learning new information, yet returning home to contexts and social structures where they felt powerless to enact change.

Addressing this lack of critical reflection on empathy is important, because empathy 'can also have negative consequences, so attention must be given to maximizing its beneficial effects'.[63] In particular, Stephan and Finlay note that empathy that does not entail respect for another group is problematic and that it can result in patronising or condescending behaviour toward minority group members.[64] Similarly, as Pedwell claims, a risk exists that through immersion programmes aimed at empathy development, global development professionals may develop empathy through activities in which 'the poor "third world" "other" remains simply the object of empathy and thus once again fixed in place'.[65] In this sense, she suggests that, while empathy may be a transformative political tool, it may also be used to uphold existing hierarchies.[66] Head suggests that such outcomes may even be fostered by particular framings of empathy: 'Representing empathy ... as a benign, beneficial process of reconciliation ... contains within it the potential seeds of a hierarchical, asymmetrical relationship between the empathiser and the recipient'.[67] In this sense, the power dynamics that may be inherent in the process of empathising must be recognised. Indeed, some dance artists have chosen to focus on their own artistic practice rather than engaging in further cultural exchanges as they are frustrated by the continued experience of asymmetric power and lack of visible change.[68]

It is also important to understand the context and translation of empathy in different cultures and languages. For example, during the field research in the Philippines, a relationship between verbal and nonverbal definitions of empathy was noted. In Visayan, the main language spoken in Mindanao, there is no single-word translation for empathy. Discussions with the local participants determined the phrase 'feeling *sa pagsinati sa gibati uban*'. This evolved and finally become '*pagtugkad sa gibati sa uban*'. The former means 'experiencing the feelings of others' while the latter means 'deepening the experience of the feelings of others'. Translating word for word the idiom 'putting yourself into the shoes of others' to describe empathy does not make sense in the Filipino context, because while Filipino culture contains high levels of perception and action around empathy, the concept of shoes is foreign. Many people do not have shoes or wear only slippers (*tsinelas*, sandals). According to interviewees, shoes are viewed as being very formal, for special occasions. These nuances highlight the role of language, symbols and embodiment in relation to empathy.

In some contexts, empathy can result in unwanted consequences such as defensive avoidance, increased distance between groups, the confirmation of negative stereotypes, negative attitudes, hurt feelings, greater hostility and tension, or reduced self-esteem.[69] Moreover, prospects for empathy to support positive peace with social justice can be blunted where they create compassion without simultaneously enabling the actors involved to see how 'they themselves are implicated in the social forces responsible for the suffering with which they are empathizing'.[70] Likewise, 'trainers, facilitators and educators may have to raise these issues explicitly and insist that participants treat each other with respect'.[71]

Going further, Pedwell suggests that 'acknowledgement of complicity is essential to any form of empathetic engagement with the potential to play a role in radically disrupting existing power relations'.[72] With this in mind, it is important to recognise that the meaning attributed to empathy can be context specific, given that it is created and embedded in particular political and cultural environments.[73] Creating empathy in the context of sustainably transforming relationships can also take a long time and requires ongoing engagement.[74] In the context of self-care for peacebuilding practitioners, it is also important to understand the possibilities of compassion fatigue when continually engaging with others in conflict or trauma. Keeping these caveats in mind, the following section explores whether and how empathy may have been fostered through the use of dance and creative movement in the peacebuilding initiatives studied for this book.

Mirroring and the empathy connection

According to Alexander and LeBaron: 'Dance and movement can open up and strengthen underused channels of communication, giving us ways to engage with one another at kinaesthetic, nonverbal levels.'[75] Further, they suggest that embodied practices can foster trust and flexibility, which may prove effective in conflict settings.[76] This can include links to embodied experiences and interpretations of emotions in relation to self and others, and mirroring is one way to explore this phenomenon. Understandings based on neuroscience have linked the embodied practice of mirroring and the activation of mirror neurons to empathy.[77]

An increasingly popular area of research, the discovery of mirror neurons led to new ways of understanding how actions are generated, as well as how we observe and interpret the actions of others. Mirror neurons adapt their activity when an individual executes a specific motor act or gesture, as well as when they observe the same or a similar act or gesture performed by another individual.[78] They are activated in an individual who is merely witnessing another person performing an action, gesture or expression of emotion.[79] Perceiving the action of another person activates the same brain areas in the observer as though one is performing the action oneself. Mirror neurons create an embodied simulation that sponsors our capacity to share actions, emotions and intentions with others.[80] For example, this may explain why an audience member sways along while watching a performer on stage, or feels a strong physical and emotional connection to a partner in a dance activity.[81] Mirror neurons have been linked to empathy, as they react to movements, sounds, facial expressions and gestures or intentions of movement, and form a sophisticated, nuanced system for shared coding of actions of self and others.[82]

Finding empathy, practising peace through dance

Research has shown that action execution and observation are linked processes, and our motor systems are involved in the interpretation of others' actions.[83] Research has also shown a connection between the motor system and cognitive function. In addition to the control and production of movement, neurons are involved in coding peripersonal space, or the space around our bodies where we interact with the environment.[84] Behrends, Müller and Dziobek link the deliberate practice of imitation and mirroring to differentiation of the self from others and extrapolate these interactions as leading to greater social integration, affiliation and agency.[85] They further suggest the value of self-perceptive tasks and creative movement fostering the basis for empathetic interaction.[86] Extending these concepts to the context of IR and diplomacy, Holmes suggests that mirror neurons may be linked to the emphasis that diplomats and leaders place on face-to-face meetings and the understanding of the intentions of others.[87]

Despite the popularity and public interest in the concept of mirror neurons, it is important to critically analyse any claims surrounding mirror neurons and the connections to empathy. Overall there is limited research with humans; the results remain connected to the rest of the brain's information-processing systems rather than being isolated, and the links to empathy are complex.[88] Critics question the relationship of mirror neurons to action understanding, the transferability of the original studies with macaques to applications in the arts, and whether the function of mirror neurons may be imitation rather than action understanding.[89] Further, empathy does not necessarily require the mirror neuron faculty.[90] In some cases, it is assumed that empathy will resolve antisocial actions, despite scientific research suggesting that empathy still exists within a framework of ideology, propaganda, culture, tradition, prejudice and in-group bias.[91]

While keeping such limits in mind, we believe that extending the mirroring concept to that of embodied practice is worthwhile, since links have been made by those working in the field of psychotherapy who are utilising mirroring as an aspect of DMT, with scholars predicting that this practice 'will enhance empathic understanding and that it will be most effective with music'.[92] Beyond this, in more everyday applications without a therapeutic aim, mirroring is also linked to empathy and to prospects for peacebuilding.

Mirroring is used in a range of dance contexts, including in some peacebuilding resources, which incorporate mirroring as an icebreaker activity. Many prospects for peace have been theorised to emerge from practices of mirroring. For example, Beausoleil argues that mirroring helps us to understand others and is thus integral to empathy, explaining that as similar bodily states are incited in the observer he or she gains greater accuracy in interpreting the emotions of the other.[93] Moreover, she says, our capacity to move with others is deeply connected to our capacity to feel with them, 'and our bodies, in turn, move in response to such feelings'.[94] Thus, mirroring, she says, 'is a shortcut to empathy'.[95] The empathy she speaks of is an embodied identification, or kinaesthetic empathy. Beausoleil claims: 'The firing of identical motor neurons when observing others gives us what is effectively firsthand experience from which to understand and empathize with them.'[96] Alexander and LeBaron expand on the concept of kinaesthetic empathy, suggesting that dance increases kinaesthesia – or being aware of one's own body, as well as the bodies of others – and proposing that 'learning about the subtle cues, demands and tendencies of one's own body has been linked to understanding empathy, or how other moving bodies might feel'.[97]

At the same time, the prospects for mirroring and empathy likely go beyond one-on-one encounters, particularly when considering that coordinated movement has been linked with empathy more generally.[98] In this context, some scholars have spoken of learning choreography as mirroring.[99] Therefore, it is possible to conceive of both doing and following choreography as a practice of mirroring that enables empathy and that potentially contributes to fostering peacebuilding.

Finding empathy, practising peace through dance

In the particular programmes we worked with for this study, across all three case study sites, one-on-one and group mirroring activities including eye contact were a central aspect of the programming. Some participants in the Philippines described the experience of mirroring as follows:

> [In the] mirror exercise you need to copy what your partner is doing. You need to copy their movement. So, I'm very excited to copy her movement. For me, eye-to-eye contact is very important, if you are going to see eye to eye, [it] is just like you are listening to that person … you and your partner will realise that you are following each other and that you both have developed respect with one another. ('Ben', Philippines)

> It was so fun. It's like … any movement you make your partner follows you. For example, if I raise my hand, my partner repeats what I'm doing. I can feel that there's a mirror in front of me. ('MJ', Philippines)

> In the workshop we had the mirror exercise wherein you come face to face with your partner, your facial and eye expression is like seeing yourself through the mirror. It is like reflecting to your own emotions and expressions. ('Bea', Philippines)

Reflecting on the mirroring exercises they engaged in through the M4P programme, participants described a variety of feelings and experiences around understanding others, or developing respect and empathy, as well as simply having fun:

> I think there's a communication between you and your partner and maybe you can tell someone what his attitudes through his movements are. If he's very smooth in doing movement, maybe … this guy is very relaxed and not tense. Things like that … For me it's great because it teaches you how to follow movements, it teaches you how to respect another person even if you don't know that person well, but then you have to respect her or his movements. ('Franc', Philippines)

> Your partner is going to follow your movement and vice versa. You and your partner will realise that you are following each other and that you both have developed respect with one another. So, I'm happy to do that … and then in the mirror exercise it is very exciting because in that activity you can see the inner aspect of that person through their eyes … If you look in the eye of a person if they do something like glancing away, you can see or say that he or she is shy. Then, if you look directly to their eyes [and] he or she responded, I will think that he or she is very proud and [a] good listener, and then they respect you. ('Ben', Philippines)

> Overall, I observed that they all had fun, they enjoyed the mirror activity, and gained friends especially with their partners. ('Jesza', Philippines)

At the same time, participants across the programmes noted many limits or challenges that might arise in the use of the mirroring activity as it was deployed in the programmes studied, including that the approach might not be accessible or appropriate for some people based on their feelings, personality, physical abilities or religious beliefs. As some young Filipino women said of mirroring:

> At first it's very hard to maintain eye contact [with] a person you don't know. You will feel like you're insecure or … something like that. But then I have this message from the brain that you have to do it … As we go along, I get used to it. Maintaining eye contact is never easy but then it could be harsh for some, but it could be okay to some. I've [got] used to doing mirror exercise. And seeing others – others feel uncomfortable. I know how it feels to be uncomfortable doing it for the first time but as you get along, as you get to know the person, there are improvements. ('Mirabelle', Philippines)

> It's very hard. I'm not fond of having eye contact with another person but [M4P] really taught me to do that. In that very moment I start liking making eye contact [with] someone. And making eye contact [with] someone you think that you feel and you see what's on their mind. ('April', Philippines)

Finding empathy, practising peace through dance

> From my experience, it feels great to see that my partner can copy correctly my movements but it also feels awful if they cannot copy. I have a perception that if they cannot copy your movement there must be something wrong or I can't be a good leader. For me, if I am the follower, I will try to imitate correctly because I don't want them to have thoughts about me of not being serious or interested in the activities. Through that mirror activity you can learn how to respect others as well as yourself. ('Jesza', Philippines)

Similarly, a young Colombian woman explained:

> I think that the curriculum is difficult for children who haven't expressed their feelings. In Colombia the people dance a lot, but don't use the movement to express themselves like yoga or something like that, that you can feel your body and can have a different relationship with your body … I think that [M4P] needs some of that; for example, the mirrors, the first four classes the teenagers can't do that because they feel very uncomfortable, they started to laugh, and it was very difficult. I think it was one of the biggest challenges for implementing [M4P] in Colombia, and in those backgrounds … the children don't have that opportunity to relate in a different way with their bodies; and [M4P] starts [at] a level that the teenagers don't have, because they haven't had the opportunities to explore that type of movement. ('Camila', Colombia)

Moreover, while these young peacebuilders described how people might feel personally uncomfortable in the mirroring activity based on the activity itself, others noted that challenges may arise around how different people are situated in relation to the activity. As one young Filipino man said:

> In a mirror exercise … we need to have an eye-to-eye contact, right? And then … some other religion[s], especially the Muslims, cannot do the eye-to-eye contact. It is prohibited for them to see the eye, especially from a man [to] a woman. So, if they have eye-to-eye contact they cannot allow them to do it … Another example … it would be difficult and hard for [somebody] to do the activity because of his disability. So, it's hard to manage, especially if in one room

there's different diversity, attitude, and some will need special attention to be given to them. ('Ben', Philippines)

A young Colombian woman explained that limits can occur where mirroring activities are not being clearly linked to related discussions around peacebuilding:

> The mirror, that is one of the main exercises of [M4P], I can't imagine [being] in a conflict and [saying to] the other people, 'Stop, let's do that'. I don't think that it could have any result. I think it's another of the challenges of [M4P] … is that you have an emphasis on movement, another part of the session is, like, let's go to talk about conflict resolution, conflict transformation and empathy, anger management; but I think that sometimes you don't have a link between those things. For example, you can use the same mirror for the talk of anger management or conflict transformation – they are very different things – but the curriculum doesn't use the movement in a way that the activity of movement that you are doing has a direct relationship with the topic you are talking [about], and I felt that with so many things … I think that the curriculum needs still more work, in order to make a daily link between those things. ('Camila', Colombia)

These participants are describing the ways in which through mirroring they were able to see different perspectives of themselves and others as well as the challenges they saw to achieving such outcomes. While US participants were less likely to speak directly about mirroring as a practice in particular, they also commonly noted the way working with M4P had changed their view of others and of themselves in the process. When asked to elaborate on how this had occurred, some explained:

> I think it has really forced me to see everybody as a potential partner, or dancer or participant in programming or participant in the communicative process. I think that before [M4P], in theory I was very … interested in … how the arts can be used to … include other people and be a force in our society, but because I had … so much … training geared towards being … professional in the

performing arts I was very limited in my ability to see someone before and say that they could dance. I had a very ... almost elite view of it ... it's expanded my thinking in that who can participate in art ... how and why, what [art] can be used for, and so I feel ... I have more space in my life now, for education programmes and programmes like [M4P] and that they are significant and valid. It doesn't just have to be about ... what a professional artist is doing ... it's also about what kids are doing in a classroom, and about kids building techniques. ('Makayla', United States)

It's given me really valuable experience as a teacher in terms of how to deal with conflicts and anger, and it has given me opportunities to practise all of the stuff that I've learned in school about peace education and critical pedagogy, and kind of asked, 'Does this work or doesn't it?' And really be reflective in my classroom ... It has definitely caused me to ask questions, do I hold stereotypes or do I really believe ... that this potential is in a student? And if I do, how does that impact my action? ('Lily', United States)

I like to think I am already a pretty empathetic person but it reinforces how I like to approach situations working with other people, which is I really do my best to understand where it is that they are coming from and then to use that to my advantage even if it is kind of just letting them think what they want to think. ... So, learning to read people ... I think is something that I do naturally but [M4P] kind of helps reinforce that that is how we learn to get along is by understanding ourselves and each other. ('Kaylee', United States)

Conclusion

In this chapter we have critically engaged with existing literature and our own original research data to explore a few key themes. First, we suggested that connecting with and expressing emotions is a vital aspect of peacebuilding. Second, we proposed that one key aspect of this emotional engagement or expression can be accessed through empathy and that considering embodied approaches such as dance and creative movement can facilitate that process. In particular, we explored how mirroring, when done thoughtfully and when it allows space for critical reflection, can support the development of empathy and likewise the practice of peacebuilding.

At the same time, we have also highlighted limits and challenges to studying and practising empathy in the pursuit of peace, as well as how these challenges were addressed (or not) in the case study sites where we conducted our research. For example, in these case studies the practice of mirroring provided a physical way to practise empathy, yet it also raised questions about cultural appropriateness and physical abilities, issues that were not always adequately considered or addressed. Through exploring these tensions, we have made a case for allowing for emotion in peacebuilding without sidelining faculties of critical reasoning. Instead we suggest that not only are the two not dichotomous, but rather both are necessary for the pursuit of social justice – a key element of positive peace.

Notes

1 N. Head, 'Tango: the intimate dance of conflict transformation', OpenDemocracy (22 August 2013), available at: www.opendemocracy.net/en/transformation/tango-intimate-dance-of-conflict-transformation/ (accessed 14 October 2019).
2 *Ibid.*
3 E. Hutchison, *Affective Communities in World Politics: Collective Emotions after Trauma* (Cambridge: Cambridge University Press, 2016), p. xi.
4 C. Pedwell, 'Affective (self-) transformations: empathy, neoliberalism and international development', *Feminist Theory*, 13 (2012), p. 171.
5 D. Mills, *Dance and Politics: Moving Beyond Boundaries* (Manchester: Manchester University Press, 2017), p. 24.
6 Pedwell, 'Affective (self-) transformations', p. 176.
7 Hutchison, *Affective Communities in World Politics*, p. 4.
8 C. Mouffe, *Agonistics: Thinking the World Politically* (London and New York: Verso, 2013), p. 97.
9 N. Premaratna and R. Bleiker, 'Art and peacebuilding: how theatre transforms conflict in Sri Lanka', in *Palgrave Advances in Peacebuilding: Critical Developments and Approaches*, ed. by O. P. Richmond (Basingstoke: Palgrave Macmillan, 2010), pp. 376–91; L. J. Pruitt, *Youth Peacebuilding: Music, Gender, and Change* (Albany: State University of New York (SUNY) Press, 2013).
10 A. Behrends, S. Müller and I. Dziobek, 'Moving in and out of synchrony: a concept for a new intervention fostering empathy through interactional

movement and dance', *The Arts in Psychotherapy*, 39 (2012), p. 112; Head, 'Tango'.
11 B. Ehrenreich, *Dancing in the Streets: A History of Collective Joy* (London: Granta Publications, 2007), p. 24.
12 *Ibid.*
13 Mouffe, *Agonistics*, p. 96.
14 A. Grau, 'Why people dance – evolution, sociality and dance', *Dance, Movement and Spiritualities*, 2 (2015), pp. 241, 248.
15 E. Beausoleil, 'Dance and neuroscience: implications for conflict transformation', in *The Choreography of Resolution*, ed. by M. LeBaron, C. MacLeod and A. F. Acland (Chicago: American Bar Association, Section of Dispute Resolution, 2013), p. 59.
16 *Ibid.* p. 78.
17 N. Alexander and M. LeBaron, 'Dancing to the rhythm of the role-play: applying dance intelligence to conflict resolution', *Hamline Journal of Public Law and Policy*, 33 (2012), pp. 327–62; T. Ney and E. Humber, 'Dance as metaphor: the metaphor of dance and peace building', in *The Choreography of Resolution*, ed. by M. LeBaron, C. MacLeod and A. F. Acland (Chicago: American Bar Association, Section of Dispute Resolution, 2013), pp. 81–108.
18 Beausoleil, 'Dance and neuroscience', p. 69.
19 O. Ramsbotham, 'Conflict resolution in art and popular culture', in *Contemporary Conflict Resolution*, ed. by O. Ramsbotham, H. Miall and T. Woodhouse (Cambridge: Polity, 2011), p. 349.
20 Premaratna and Bleiker, 'Art and peacebuilding', p. 385.
21 Beausoleil, 'Dance and neuroscience', p. 69.
22 W. G. Stephan and K. A. Finlay, 'The role of empathy in improving intergroup relations', *Journal of Social Issues*, 55 (1999), p. 89.
23 N. Alexander and M. LeBaron, 'Embodied conflict resolution: resurrecting roleplay-based curricula through dance', in *Educating Negotiators for a Connected World*, ed. by C. Honeyman, J. Coben and A. Wei-Min Lee (Saint Paul: DRI Press, 2013), p. 550.
24 N. Head, 'A politics of empathy: encounters with empathy in Israel and Palestine', *Review of International Studies*, 42 (2016), p. 96.
25 K. Swick, 'Preventing violence through empathy development in families', *Early Childhood Education Journal*, 33 (2005), p. 53.
26 D. P. Sams and S. D. Truscott, 'Empathy, exposure to community violence, and use of violence among urban, at-risk adolescents', *Child and Youth Care Forum*, 33 (2004), p. 34.
27 D. Jolliffe and D. P. Farrington, 'Examining the relationship between low empathy and bullying', *Aggressive Behavior*, 32 (2006), p. 540.
28 Stephan and Finlay, 'The role of empathy in improving intergroup relations', p. 730.
29 Pedwell, 'Affective (self-) transformations', p. 165.

30 Head, 'A politics of empathy', p. 102.
31 *Ibid.*, p. 99.
32 *Ibid.*, p. 103.
33 *Ibid.*, p. 95.
34 *Ibid.*; Premaratna and Bleiker, 'Art and peacebuilding'.
35 M. Abu-Nimer, 'Toward the theory and practice of positive approaches to peacebuilding', in *Positive Approaches to Peacebuilding: A Resource for Innovators*, ed. by C. Sampson *et al.* (Washington DC: PACT Publications, 2003), p. 15.
36 Head, 'A politics of empathy', pp. 104, 107.
37 *Ibid.*, p. 109.
38 *Ibid.*, p. 105.
39 Swick, 'Preventing violence', p. 54.
40 *Ibid.*
41 *Ibid.*, pp. 56, 58.
42 Sams and Truscott, 'Empathy, exposure to community violence', p. 37.
43 Swick, 'Preventing violence', p. 53.
44 Jolliffe and Farrington, 'Examining the relationship between low empathy and bullying', p. 547.
45 Sams and Truscott, 'Empathy, exposure to community violence', p. 33.
46 *Ibid.*, p. 36.
47 Behrends, Müller and Dziobek, 'Moving in and out of synchrony', p. 112.
48 P. D. Facci, 'On human potential: peace and conflict transformation fostered through dance' (Master's dissertation, Universitat Innsbruck, 2011), p. 89.
49 G. Monbiot, *Out of the Wreckage: A New Politics for an Age of Crisis* (London and New York: Verso, 2017), p. 9.
50 Swick, 'Preventing violence', p. 58.
51 Stephan and Finlay, 'The role of empathy in improving intergroup relations', p. 729.
52 *Ibid.*, pp. 730–1.
53 *Ibid.*, p. 735.
54 K. A. Finlay and W. G. Stephan, 'Improving intergroup relations: the effects of empathy on racial attitudes', *Journal of Applied Social Psychology*, 30 (2000), p. 1734.
55 Stephan and Finlay, 'The role of empathy in improving intergroup relations', p. 738.
56 Pedwell, 'Affective (self-) transformations', p. 163.
57 *Ibid.*, p. 164.
58 Head, 'A politics of empathy', p. 97.
59 Pedwell, 'Affective (self-) transformations', p. 164.
60 *Ibid.*, p. 166.
61 Head, 'A politics of empathy', p. 96.

62 C. Lamm and J. Majdandzic, 'The role of shared neural activations, mirror neurons, a morality in empathy – a critical comment', *Neuroscience Research*, 90 (2015), pp. 14–24.
63 Stephan and Finlay, 'The role of empathy in improving intergroup relations', p. 740.
64 *Ibid.*, p. 737.
65 Pedwell, 'Affective (self-) transformations', p. 172.
66 *Ibid.*, p. 166.
67 Head, 'A politics of empathy', p. 101.
68 R. Buck, N. Rowe, and R. Martin, *Talking Dance: Contemporary Histories from the Southern Mediterranean* (London: I.B. Tauris, 2014).
69 Stephan and Finlay, 'The role of empathy in improving intergroup relations', p. 739.
70 *Ibid.*
71 *Ibid.*, p. 737.
72 Pedwell, 'Affective (self-) transformations', p. 173.
73 Head, 'A politics of empathy', p. 102.
74 *Ibid.*, p. 104.
75 N. Alexander and M. LeBaron, 'Building kinesthetic intelligence: dance in conflict-resolution education', in *The Choreography of Resolution*, ed. by M. LeBaron, C. MacLeod and A. F. Acland (Chicago: American Bar Association, Section of Dispute Resolution, 2013), p. 231.
76 *Ibid.*, p. 238.
77 C. Berrol, 'Neuroscience meets dance/movement therapy: mirror neurons, the therapeutic process and empathy', *The Arts in Psychotherapy*, 33 (2006), pp. 302–15.
78 G. Rizzolatti *et al.*, 'Premotor cortex and the recognition of motor actions', *Cognitive Brain Research*, 3 (1996), pp. 131–41.
79 M. Reason and D. Reynolds, 'Kinesthesia, empathy, and related pleasures: an inquiry into audience experiences of watching dance', *Dance Research Journal*, 42 (2010), p. 50.
80 V. Gallese, 'Mirror neurons, embodied simulation, and the neural basis of social identification', *Psychoanalytic Dialogues*, 19 (2009), p. 520.
81 D. Freedberg and V. Gallese, 'Motion, emotion and empathy in esthetic experience', *Trends in Cognitive Sciences*, 11 (2007), p. 197.
82 G. Rizzolatti and L. Craighero, 'The mirror-neuron system', *Annual Review of Neuroscience*, 27 (2004), pp. 169–92.
83 J. Kilner and R. Lemon, 'What we know currently about mirror neurons', *Current Biology*, 23 (2013), pp. R1057–62.
84 P. F. Ferrari and G. Rizzolatti, 'Mirror neuron research: the past and the future', *Philosophical Transactions of the Royal Society B: Biological Sciences*, 369 (2014), https://doi.org/10.1098/rstb.2013.0169.
85 Behrends, Müller and Dziobek, 'Moving in and out of synchrony'.

86 *Ibid.*
87 M. Holmes, 'The force of face-to-face diplomacy: mirror neurons and the problem of intentions', *International Organization*, 67 (2013), pp. 829–61.
88 C. F. Alford, 'Mirror neurons, psychoanalysis, and the age of empathy', *International Journal of Applied Psychoanalytic Studies*, 13 (2016), pp. 7–23.
89 D. Davies, 'Dancing around the issues: prospects for an empirically grounded philosophy of dance', *Journal of Aesthetics and Art Criticism*, 71 (2013), pp. 198–201.
90 Lamm and Majdandzic, 'The role of shared neural activations'.
91 J. Y. Chiao and V. A. Mathur, 'Intergroup empathy: how does race affect empathic neural responses?', *Current Biology*, 20 (2010), pp. R478–80.
92 L. M. McGarry and F. A. Russo, 'Mirroring in dance/movement therapy: potential mechanisms behind empathy enhancement', *The Arts in Psychotherapy*, 38 (2011), p. 183.
93 Beausoleil, 'Dance and neuroscience', p. 70.
94 *Ibid.*
95 *Ibid.*, p. 72.
96 *Ibid.*, p. 71.
97 Alexander and LeBaron, 'Dancing to the rhythm of the role-play', p. 350.
98 Behrends, Müller and Dziobek, 'Moving in and out of synchrony', p. 112.
99 McGarry and Russo, 'Mirroring in dance/movement therapy'.

5
Embodying peace: prospects for self-care within settings of conflict

> *If I were to think about the times in my life when I feel like I've encountered peace, it's sort of this very tangible experience of wholeness or of right relationship with your environment or with other people, and also sort of with yourself, a sense of being in a place, and then here comes absence, maybe with freedom from want, freedom from anxiety, freedom from worry, and then ... things like the presence of trust and the presence of mercy and the presence of justice, which are all sort of like ephemeral things or ... intangible things. But I think I would say it's the presence of ... wholeness.*
>
> 'Lily', M4P facilitator, United States

As explored in the previous chapters, when asked how they define or understand peace, our research participants regularly noted that it was about being in nonviolent, just relationships with others at a variety of levels. Questions of the self are also central in these understandings, including how one interacts with and relates to others. Participants in each of the countries visited for this study situated the self as key in their conceptions of peace. Many felt peace had to start in the self or could not be sustainable; for them, peace needed to be maintained at a personal, as well as a relational, level. When explaining how they defined or understood peace, many participants referred to the centrality of knowing the self, being aware of the self, and feeling confident, or at least relaxed or safe in one's own physical body.

Likewise, we believe these themes deserve more investigation in the service of peacebuilding, so we aim to begin that journey in this chapter. To date, practitioner self-care is underexplored in Peace and Conflict Studies, even though peacebuilders themselves could benefit immensely from further enquiry in this area, which could in turn strengthen the depth and quality of their work as facilitators for peace. Indeed, the research for this book has suggested that, through dance and creative movement, participants had an opportunity to experience themselves in a way that enabled them to express a deeper sense of self-understanding, embodiment and strength to go on with their work for peace.

In this chapter, we consider how, in the midst of difficult work in circumstances of conflict, peacebuilders have appreciated the opportunities that dance provides to relieve stress and re-engage with their bodies. At the same time, acknowledging that diverse bodies may be placed differently in settings of conflict, we also interrogate the prospects and challenges posed by gender and age norms in particular sites of peacebuilding. We suggest that dance has broader implications in peacebuilding because dance can help enable a more reflective stance for considering conflict and thus may offer new, creative directions for pursuing peace.

Knowing the self, respecting the self: implications for peacebuilding

As Lederach explains: 'When we attempt to eliminate the personal, we lose sight of ourselves, our deeper intuition, and the source of our understandings – *who we are* and *how we are* in the world.'[1] In short, the personal – the self – matters for peace. As articulated in this chapter, self-knowledge, self-esteem and self-care may play important roles in contributing to peaceful change that goes far beyond the self. Indeed, as Lederach further suggests, one key challenge of peacebuilding 'is to combine a sense of meaningful contribution and place with intentional recognition that we are part of a larger whole'.[2] Moreover, he says, listening to one's own voice is intimately connected to the ability to listen to others. This suggests 'that people who listen the best and deepest to others are those who have found a way to be in touch with their own voices'.[3] After all, the body is central to meaning-making and is a vital component of discourse.[4]

Self-knowledge, or self-acceptance, then, appears to be a key area of development for peacebuilders. After all, it is the self that connects with the wider actual or hoped-for culture of peace, and self-awareness has been linked to the ability to create change. Beausoleil, for example, highlights dance's links to developing neuroplasticity, which contributes to proprioception, and related capacities, which are linked to self-perception and agency.[5] Likewise, through contributing to enhanced neuroplasticity, Beausoleil argues that dance can 'expand our self-awareness and ability to create change in the contexts where change is needed',[6] including in conflict-affected settings where peacebuilding is required. For example, research shows that when engaging in dance, children from diverse cultural backgrounds demonstrate better understanding of each other and improved capacity to work through conflict.[7]

Relatedly, researchers have suggested that self-awareness is a requisite for empathy, alongside self–other relational awareness. Indeed, recognising and expressing one's own feelings is the foundation people require for developing understanding and relationships with others.[8] This process works in complex, multidirectional ways. For example, researchers have identified that children who do not develop empathy are often prone to not only antisocial behaviours, but also behaviours of self-harm.[9] On the other hand, empathy is correlated with leadership development, which may be directed towards addressing injustices due to empathising with those receiving unfair treatment.[10] Hence, supporting the development of self-awareness contributes not only to the self but also to fostering social relations underpinning peace.

Peacebuilders engaging in dance can contribute to 'accepting oneself, acknowledging complexity and chaos, [and] feeling part of the whole'.[11] In other words, in addressing power imbalances that may foster conflict, it is crucial to include efforts at 'recognizing and mobilizing personal and collective action'.[12] In this context, researchers have noted the prospects for dance as an avenue for expressing oneself as part of engaging in dialogue, a key facet of peacebuilding.[13] Through dance, embodied and relational aspects of dialogue may be particularly well supported. Such capacity for engagement and community also clearly relates to the participant's sense of self-esteem, which in this study appeared as a key factor of how participants felt dance had supported their engagement in peacebuilding.

Connections between self-esteem and peacebuilding also reflect previous research linking these themes, including in relation to dance. For example, Swick suggests that, just as self-awareness and empathy are connected, so too are self-esteem and empathy.[14] Moreover, Facci reported that, in observing her students she noticed them getting in touch with their bodies and enhancing confidence and self-esteem.[15] Jeffrey described a shift in self-esteem, with participants reporting feeling more connected with their own bodies, and being both more relaxed and energised.[16]

Participants in our research also expressed a sense of acceptance and increased confidence through a chance to experience their bodies in a different way. This sense of self-awareness was heightened, especially for those who previously felt like they did not have the 'right' body type or experience to be a dancer, or the permission to explore dance. Such outcomes may be crucial for moving confidently in the direction of peace. After all, research has found that 'self-efficacy beliefs were a negative predictor of violent behavior'.[17]

From our research it certainly appears that the dance-based peacebuilding approach had important outcomes in relation to confidence and self-esteem; many of the young people interviewed reported relevant changes in how they see themselves:

> [M4P] has boosted my self-confidence. I am now more comfortable in speaking with others. … Before, I was really shy, I [couldn't] communicate well with others, I [didn't] talk too much. ('Art', Philippines)

> For me … In the time that I [was] not yet with this organisation, I [was so] quiet and the people [saw] me as not approachable. So, [since I've been] within the organisation there has been a big change for me. Because every time I [see] them, I smile. My friends are telling me now that I am more approachable. ('Ben', Philippines)

> [M4P] has empowered me and enabled me to do a number of things that I probably wouldn't have had the confidence to do had I not been involved in the organisation. ('Lily', United States)

With this in mind, and building on the ideas of self-knowledge and self-esteem, self-care arises as an important area for further investigation in relation to peacebuilding. After all, there is growing research regarding anxiety levels and post-traumatic stress disorder for humanitarian workers in conflict areas, especially those who are engaged in the work for a period of longer than six months.[18] Concerns for worker wellbeing have prompted calls for organisations to focus on building resilience and elements of self-care and mental health for their employees.[19]

The value of self-care has been recognised in the work of women human rights defenders, informed by a feminist perspective; they assert that women human rights defenders have a right to enjoy pleasure and embodiment.[20] Organisations such as IM-Defensoras and Consorcio Oaxaca created and implemented self-care principles as well as opening Casa La Serena, a safe space for human rights defenders to rest, de-stress and recharge.[21] The self-care and wellness of peace practitioners is an important consideration that ties in with impact, safety and sustainability. The increase in peacebuilder and development worker self-care courses and retreats demonstrates the considered value of these approaches.

Not all of these options are available to practitioners working in all settings, and broader access warrants further consideration. However, what remains clear is that self-care is relevant for peacebuilders across a variety of contexts. To put it briefly, as one research participant from the Philippines explained:

> You cannot be a peacebuilder … if [you] cannot find peace within yourself. So, it must really start within you as an individual person. For example, I started learning the basics as being [an M4P facilitator] and I'm trying hard to maintain it at the same level until reaching [the] highest level of being a good peace advocate. ('Ben', Philippines)

Caring for the self: an underexplored yet critical element of peacebuilding

Through critically analysing existing literature and observing and interviewing the research participants, we have identified a range of ways in which dance can play fruitful roles in self-care and can likewise support peacebuilding. As Irvine asserts: 'Dance is, of course, its own justification. You dance for fun and joy, out of exuberance and energy.'[22] Allowing space for such activities for peacebuilders is important, not least because conflict transformation requires 'empathy for oneself and for the other'.[23]

At the same time, the feelings provoked by dance can offer important resources for peacebuilders. As Facci says, in reflecting on her own practice: 'Dancing always brought warmth to my heart, strength to my will, and determination to my challenges.'[24] Other researchers in a range of contexts have also noted that practitioners working in peacebuilding or conflict transformation can gain benefits of self-healing through the practice of creative activities such as theatre, and particularly dance.[25] Similarly, Eddy argues that dance can facilitate relaxation and the resilience required to return the body to a relaxed state when needed.[26] This resonates with Siapno's suggestion that dance can be used to foster resilience, including in everyday and post-conflict settings, and can promote 'care-of-the-self', which she links to embodied presence.[27] Furthermore, she describes how practices of performing arts can offer 'an embodied site for individuals and communities to re-emerge as active agents in their resilience and recovery', even within the context of power inequalities between the local and international.[28]

Overall, the existing literature suggests that the capacity for dance to contribute to self-awareness, self-esteem and self-care in support of peacebuilding is an important area that needs more investigation. Statements from participants regarding their understandings of peace lent support to the exploration of these concepts. They start with their own awareness and radiate outwards to others. For example, our research participants explained how they define peace as follows:

> I think it starts with an individual, you know, finding inner peace, and I think that … means something different to everyone … I think it's the ability to kind of accept what's happening around you and knowing like, if you're trying your best or you are content with your efforts and your place in life, then you know that's a way to find sort of inner peace … I feel that can ripple throughout society, so you start with the inner peace at the individual and then you find interpersonal peace and … that's kind of like the idea of peace that I have in terms of for myself and then for a larger community or ultimately the world. ('Emily', United States)

> My favourite way of thinking about peace is kind of like concentric circles, holistic models. So, peace exists within the self and may be first within the self and in expanding rings outward from there. So, within the self, in small groups, within a community, in schools, in families, in societies, in the world and even thinking of our stewardship of the earth and natural resources as one part of what peace is. ('Emma', United States)

Peace means there's no violence. And it means peace within me. ('MJ', Philippines)

Peace means … having no misunderstandings. It's like having this inner peace of yourself … I can compare it with the water, very clear and calm water wherein you could think well and you could communicate well. ('Mirabelle', Philippines)

Okay, I tell you all those dreams of peace … the peace point is when you reflect, you are relaxed, but it starts from you, from deep inside, so the peace is achieved first [with] the interior peace. ('Juan', Colombia)

Peace I think is a state that we should first search [for] inside, in order to make it transmittable, to share and reproduce it in the community. ('Luciana', Colombia)

In the following sections we explore some key ways these themes were identified and explained by research participants in our study. Reflecting back on these issues and taking them further with explorations of key sub-themes around managing stress, relaxing, engaging physically and embodying peace, we attempt to offer some new insights for both the theory and practice of peacebuilding through the lens of dance.

Self-care may be particularly relevant for practitioners, facilitators or participants in peacebuilding efforts, given that they may often face stressful situations and could thus benefit from practices addressing stress or relaxing in healthy ways, including through dance and creative movement activities. Likewise, Beausoleil has argued that dance can assist legal practitioners who work in conflict transformation by contributing to their resilience in sustained, complex settings of stress.[29] Moreover, she notes that stress, shame or threats can lead to the body producing chemicals which can limit blood flow to the brain,[30] so addressing these factors may assist in clearer thinking in the pursuit of peace. Likewise, many of our research participants made links between addressing stress, dance and peacebuilding:

> Dance is very important if you're going to relieve your stress ... you want to exercise ... we need to move, stretch our body to release the stress. So, peace and dance [have] a connection between them. ('Ben', Philippines)

> I believe that with dance ... it helps release stress and other feelings that can make a person violent. ('Valeria', Colombia)

> [Before working with M4P] I didn't understand directly how [dance for peacebuilding] would work but now I can see pretty clearly how it's allowing these kids to express themselves and release a little bit of stress and bring some joy into their lives and also kind of getting better in touch with who they are and how they feel ... [M4P] kind of helps reinforce that how we learn to get along is by understanding ourselves and each other. ('Kaylee', United States)

In terms of the capacity to relax, Eddy notes this can be fostered through dance and creative movement practices, especially when it comes to the use of breath control. In particular, she says, somatic awareness making movement conscious can hasten the process of regulating the body back into a relaxed physical condition, or homeostasis. The ability to do so quickly demonstrates resilience and fosters sustainable health. Through engaging in conscious, slow and deep breathing, for instance, a person in an anxiety-provoking situation can find calm, according to Eddy. Moreover, she notes that escalated conflict is less likely to occur where relaxation is present and stress is reduced.[31]

Facci connects such relaxation through breathing with the transformative aspect of conflict, emphasising that breathing can be key to 'making it possible to accept resonance with oneself and with others'.[32] With this capacity for breathing and relaxing may come the capacity for flexibility, innovation and an increased range of options in decision-making. Through the body these capacities are realised in physical dance terms, as well as metaphorically in terms of needed shifts in addressing conflict and violence, or what Lederach refers to as the ability 'to situate oneself in a changing environment with a sense of direction and purpose and at the same time develop an ability to see and move with the unexpected'.[33]

Such breathing practices are often also incorporated as elements within broader approaches to 'interpersonal transformation', which includes 'practices such as mediation, meditation and mindfulness' that can 'teach us to examine and manage our own emotions, stories, and judgements'.[34] Practices such as mindfulness, which aim 'to quiet the constant chatter of the left brain and activate the parasympathetic nervous system that reduces stress and increases calmness and happiness', are significant for addressing conflict and building peace, since 'entrenched patterns for thought and action, particularly in response to threat, are obstacles to the discovery of possible ways forward'.[35] Further, meditation has been linked to enhanced 'compassionate responses to suffering, even in the face of social pressures to avoid so doing'.[36]

These ideas from the literature have also been integrated to some degree in M4P's programming, which was based on the notion that dance and creative movement could assist participants with relaxing, including through teaching breathing practices as well as including final relaxation and meditation in programme sessions. As M4P's founder explained:

> So, some of the anger management strategies that we talk about in the curriculum are like five deep breaths, drinking lots of water and all of that's done through movement … So, I think that's where we're looking at empathy and the physical balance is where we talk more about anger management strategies and self-regulating, calming ourselves down when we're stressed. ('Claire', M4P founder, United States)

Noting her pointing directly to the physical aspects of the programme, it is worth exploring how physical elements have been treated in peacebuilding literature, as well as how other participants in our research engaged with the physicality of dancing for peace.

Physical as critical: let's get physical for peace?

Having discussed the emotional aspects of embodiment in greater detail, we now consider the physical aspects of embodiment in relation to dance and peacebuilding. Of course, the two cannot be completely separated. As noted in the discussion on empathy and emotion in Chapter 4, our physical states and our emotions are related, and both can move and shift, even during conflict. Both are also embodied. Likewise, Berents argues for an embodied everyday peace that 'draws on narratives and practices of resistance, resilience, collective notions of belonging, and aspirational planning for a different future'.[37]

Indeed, our bodies influence our understandings and responses in ways that go beyond processing emotions, since '[p]hysical sensation is not only the expression but also the source of emotion: the limbic system'.[38] Likewise, 'physical movement can lead to conceptual, emotional, and interpersonal shifts'.[39] Moreover, 'physical sensations and slight changes to stance, gesture, or movement can affect the emotional state of people in conflict', and new physical habits can thus aid in shifting conflicts.[40] For example, activities that include altering physical states (e.g. asking people to go for a walk) have a better chance of effectively shifting people's emotions compared to purely verbal engagement with the causes of these emotions.[41] As one of our participants from the US explained:

> Especially in a place like Washington DC … there's a lot of really physical violence that afflicts students but in school you don't necessarily see school affecting kids' way of dealing with their bodies or their control of their bodies or their control physically. I think that really any form of physical activity but especially dance can help

foster a more controlled and peaceful understanding and awareness of your physical self. And I think that ... there's also the aspect of dance as a form of expression; dance is a way to interact with others in a way that's not your traditional way of interacting with others not through verbal exchanges. ('Lily', United States)

At the same time, we recognise feminist challenges to 'the too-easy equation of subjectivity with physical embodiment', and wish to acknowledge the important role feminist research has played in interrogating 'issues of embodiment as political in order to expose how conceptions of the seemingly natural body normalize certain forms of political oppression and exclusion'.[42] After all, some of our research participants noted how, for example, based on gender and physical ability, people might be more or less likely to be safe or feel safe in public. They cited, for example, that girls faced harassment in public spaces and boys were more likely to be involved in or affected by certain types of direct violence. Likewise, some peacebuilding activities, including dance and creative movement for peace, could feel less accessible or safe to some participants, especially where conscious efforts are not made to ensure accessibility for a range of physical abilities or gender identities.

In this context, dance and conflict appear as parallel, since 'parties in conflict dance expected, rehearsed, and improvised routines/ steps as they sense, intuit, and respond to verbal and physical cues; and power (im)balances are always in operation when they are performed physically and through narrative'.[43] Indeed, peacebuilders seeking to utilise dance need to remain cautious and aware regarding the ways in which dance can be utilised as a means of reinforcing established patterns or power imbalances, for example in contexts of expressions of identity through the valorisation of national dances.[44]

While recognising such complexities and potential limitations, we do think it is important to delve into physical prospects for peacebuilding, not least because conflict itself is often physical, yet the 'physical wisdom contained in the metaphor of dance is an essential element missing from conflict theory and practice'.[45] While physical activity, including dance, typically offers a variety of benefits to health and wellbeing in general, when it comes to peacebuilding, movement may be particularly important in enabling the person moving, with a greater sense of body awareness, to feel 'more able to do a wider range of things'.[46] This would include engaging in 'conceptual, emotional, and interpersonal shifts',[47] including those that might facilitate peacebuilding. At the more personal level, being more aware of and 'listening' to the whole body can also support the mover in releasing 'traumatic memories and the physical pain associated with them'.[48]

Movement-based efforts have been shown to positively 'enable a state of open receptiveness',[49] another potential building block for peace in conflict-affected settings. Likewise, researchers have investigated the use of physical activities like dance to support violence prevention in schools, including in the US, one of the countries considered in our research.[50] Physical touch, as often occurs in partnered or group dances, for example, has been described as necessary 'to overpower the cold logic of verbal arguments and bind human communities'.[51] Similarly, as some research participants suggested:

> I think that our society at large really doesn't acknowledge the amount of knowledge that can be shared and communicated and learned through physicalising things. We're not just heads. You know, we focused so much on what goes on in our heads but … sometimes words are difficult, and moving brings people to an equal level and can unite people and build community in a much more organic and much more quick way than talking out loud. ('Emma', United States)

> I think it [dance/movement] also is really good at giving [people], and not even just youth, another avenue to express themselves, if they don't feel comfortable expressing themselves verbally, or they don't understand it verbally, you can see if physically, through really getting something into your body, you can understand what it feels

like to behave a certain way. Or how challenging it is to work in certain groups. It's sort of like, 'Wow, that's really hard and I feel uncomfortable right now.' But it gives you the tools to use in life to get past that discomfort. ('Makayla', United States)

In this way, just as it is important to interrogate prospects for understanding mind–body connections in relation to conflict transformation, it is also important to consider the relationship between communication and physical movement, not least because we mostly communicate nonverbally.[52] Like movement, communication is inevitably political. Overall, research indicates that creative, physical movement can make particularly important contributions to conflict transformation.[53]

Here we agree that 'dance provides an adaptable and accessible form of physical movement for elevating mood, energy levels, and motivation', and likewise 'dance, among the most complex of physical activities, holds particular potential to enhance mental capacity and shift affective states, both essential to transforming conflict'.[54] Overall, in the context of M4P the physicality of the programme was seen as integral to a broader, holistic approach to peacebuilding incorporating multiple perspectives. As the founder explained:

> With [M4P] we're educating the whole person. And we're doing that in a way that's integrative, that's interdisciplinary, that's not segmenting peace education and saying, 'Okay, today ... at 4 o'clock we're going to talk about conflict management and mediation and in the morning we're going to have reading and then in the afternoon we're going to have science'. [Our aim is instead to] integrate the education principles when learning about biology, when learning about chemistry, when doing world cultures ... and if you can do it in a way that's physical, it just makes it more real and holistic as you're getting the whole person. ('Claire', M4P founder, United States)

This holistic view is also useful to apply in the broader consideration of bodies. After all, as LeBaron and MacLeod argue: 'Physical

Embodying peace

bodies are sites of trauma, anchors of pain, and divisions between one group and another'; simultaneously, they 'are also vessels of possibility, vehicles of change, and places of healing'.[55]

Embodying peace

As explained in this book's introduction, bodies tend to be ignored in mainstream research looking at IR, Security Studies and other key areas contributing to Peace and Conflict Studies. As Parviainen argues, 'bodies have been used as a political tool in activism, but many scholars have ignored activists' highly sophisticated and intelligent ways of using their moving bodies'.[56] We believe this marginalisation demonstrates a lack of imagination around understanding bodies and how they matter politically, locally and globally. Recognising the need to critically engage with bodies when it comes to peacebuilding, our work is informed by Wilcox, who, by building on earlier feminist contributions, has enabled us to see bodies as produced and productive, as well as social, political and constructed.[57]

Acknowledging that bodies can be targeted for violence, we note the malleability of bodies and assert that they also hold capacity for resistance, including through producing different political identities and possibilities for peaceful interaction across difference. In doing so, bodies can generate fresh social configurations and political subjectivities. For example, dance has been used as a means to renegotiate group identity and to physically make a claim on space in the face of forced migration. The Banabans are a group of people originally from the island of Banaba, Kiribati. However, the British Phosphate Commissioners forced the Banabans off their land and relocated them to Rabi Island, Fiji. Subsequently, phosphate mining has destroyed the majority of the Banabans' ancestral home.[58] The loss of land, political conflicts and their new home on Rabi influenced the emergence of 'Banaban dance', which is now recognised by researchers and artists as a unique Pacific dance tradition.[59] As

Teaiwa explains: 'People on Rabi are actively creating their culture from all possible sources, even as they politically maintain a timeless and unchanging Banaban identity or essence. Both innovation and continuity prevail.'[60] The creation of Banaban dance became a political act to establish their identity as a group, to embody and claim their space while in a new geographic location.

Embodiment, specifically around women's bodies as a site of violence, is also used as a means of creating a counternarrative and sense of political identity. For example, at the Gathering of Nations Powwow in 2017, Tia Wood, who was named 'head young lady dancer', called for dancers to join together and bring attention to the high number of missing and murdered indigenous women in the US and Canada by wearing red dresses and performing an old-style jingle dance.[61] The dance was inspired by the work of artist Jaime Black and the REDress Project, which gathered and displayed over six hundred red dresses across Canada.[62] Wood initiated the dance as a means of healing, as well as representing a highly visible call for advocacy, honouring missing and murdered women, and activating women's bodies as a site of resistance rather than of violence.

Most attention to embodiment in IR has focused on bodies and violence, and we agree this is a centrally important area for investigation. In this study we aim to expand the field by considering relations of embodiment incorporated into efforts towards peace and conflict transformation. How might reflecting on bodies inform the ways we think about everyday practices of peace? What might they tell us about who can engage in peacebuilding, when and how? Such questions are urgent. As we live through bodies and in bodies, it is crucial to understand the complexities of how they are formed and move to facilitate creatively rethinking future political directions.[63]

Although the embodiment of the subject is political,[64] this is not accounted for in the existing emerging work considering dance and creative movement in peacebuilding. Likewise, informed by feminist researchers' contributions, we aim to expand the dialogue

Embodying peace

around dance and peacebuilding. Feminist research has a great deal to contribute to such an understanding because 'feminist research is a feminist questioning about how bodies matter politically'.[65] Feminist research allows us to consider bodies and politics, not just the 'body politic' so often the gendered focus of mainstream political enquiries. In this way, 'feminist research agendas are often tuned into stories, experiences and representations of peoples/individuals/bodies rather than states or political elites', and 'this is how feminist security studies potentially performs critical security studies differently'.[66]

Contributions by feminist researchers allow us to see important ways bodies are constituted and understood differently. This has often transpired by focusing on women or 'those bodies identified as female, precisely because such bodies have been underrepresented or represented in particular ways in global politics, but a focus on bodies also includes attention to male, intersexual, queer, transsexual, and/or raced, classed, aged, able/disabled, or in other ways "othered" and to how such categories are constructed and continuously reproduced'.[67] Indeed, participants in our research highlighted varying ways programmes using dance for peace might affect the different ways bodies are understood, produced and moved for different groups. As one young woman explained:

> The idea of the project was a type of foundation for dance … where girls could begin to value their body as well occupy their free time. ('Valeria', Colombia)

She suggested that girls might not feel good about their bodies, and they might benefit from efforts to address that dynamic. On the other hand, a young woman from the US explained her belief that at times women might feel more able to move their bodies in certain ways compared to men:

> It's easier perhaps for women to engage their bodies in ways that men would be a little bit more apprehensive to, but I think the more

women that we have on this path, the more men that we can possibly have in the future. ('Aubrey', United States)

These comments and the related research cited highlight an important point: while bodies matter both socially and culturally, as shown in the chapter addressing gender and intersectionality, the *ways* they matter and how they are identified or self-identified can differ on a variety of axes, including 'how … they are "sexed"'.[68] However, we aim to move beyond the common focus on sex binaries to instead deal with the complexities of how different bodies are produced and reproduced in the pursuit of peacebuilding and what the implications of recognising this may be, including prospects for transformation, at the individual and collective levels. One of the research participants for this study suggested precisely such an approach:

> The body is actually used as a stage for transformation [so we can ask] how we are able to generate complete actions and understand … the dynamics of the conflict. ('Mateo', Colombia)

Peacebuilding is the central area of transformation we aim to explore here, and we believe that bodies play a crucial role in the ability to make peace, not least because we can use our bodies in ways that may facilitate conflict or that may facilitate peace. If we fail to consider bodies, we will have reconfirmed limited and partial understandings of how people experience both conflict and peacebuilding. The capacities dancers embody (rhythm, imagination, relationality, curiosity, flexibility, emotionality, creativity and bodily tacit knowledge[69]) can make important contributions to addressing conflict. If we leave bodies out when considering how to address conflicts, 'we also neglect a whole realm of experience and perception, without which our understanding of what is going on whenever people meet can never be complete'.[70] Or, as some of our research participants explained it:

Embodying peace

> I feel that the body is one of the main elements used to express yourself, and that if people knew how to use it, it would be of great help. ('Valeria', Colombia)

> I think that dance is really helpful theoretically at least in impacting peacebuilding ... because it intentionally involves your understanding and your awareness of your body. ('Lily', United States)

In this way they demonstrate their views that addressing the ways people understand and express themselves is crucial to peacebuilding.

Finally, while in the previous section we dealt with physical aspects of the body, we should also point out that '[o]ur perceptions are not solely determined by immediate physical cues in our surroundings; our bodies also store and process memories, which shape and limit our perceptions and responses'.[71] These bodily memories can likewise influence how we perceive and interpret the world and how we respond to these interpretations.[72]

Conclusion

In this chapter, we have reflected on our research participants' understandings and practices of pursuing peace, exploring the central roles the self — and the body that houses, or to some degree comprises, the self — can and do play in this process. The young peacebuilders involved in this research often referred to aspects of the self as critical for peace, with many expressing that peace could only be possible or sustained if it started in or was present in the self. They further explained that self-knowledge or awareness and self-esteem could both be crucial for this process, as could the ability to feel relaxed or safe in one's own physical body. At the same time, they also provided insights on the complex ways different bodies may be placed and understood in this context.

Dancing through the dissonance

As young people around the world are increasingly taking up the work of peacebuilding, it is useful to reflect and share knowledge and approaches. These young peacebuilders provided insightful knowledge on how dance and creative movement expressed in physical and embodied ways could foster and sustain peacebuilding. In particular, self-care for peacebuilders has been underexplored, and our research suggests that dance and creative movement – as physical, embodied practices for peacebuilding – can offer an important means for fostering self-care. This may occur through practices that enable individuals involved in peace efforts to deal with stress in healthy ways and find methods to relax, breathe and re-engage with their bodies so that these peacebuilders can thus have the creativity, strength, courage and stamina to continue their crucial work, including in conflict-affected and often overwhelming circumstances.

Notes

1 J. P. Lederach, *The Moral Imagination: The Art and Soul of Building Peace* (Oxford: Oxford University Press, 2005), p. xii.
2 *Ibid.*, p. 107.
3 *Ibid.*, p. 165.
4 T. Aistrope, 'Popular culture, the body and world politics', *European Journal of International Relations*, 1 (2019), pp. 1–24.
5 E. Beausoleil, 'Dance and neuroscience: implications for conflict transformation', in *The Choreography of Resolution*, ed. by M. LeBaron, C. MacLeod and A. F. Acland (Chicago: American Bar Association, Section of Dispute Resolution, 2013), p. 66; E. Beausoleil and M. LeBaron, 'What moves us: dance and neuroscience implications for conflict approaches', *Conflict Resolution Quarterly*, 31 (2013), p. 140.
6 Beausoleil, 'Dance and neuroscience', p. 66.
7 Beausoleil and LeBaron, 'What moves us'; L. Koshland, J. Wilson and B. Wittaker, 'PEACE through dance/movement: evaluating a violence prevention program', *American Journal of Dance Therapy*, 26 (2004), pp. 69–90.
8 K. Swick, 'Preventing violence through empathy development in families', *Early Childhood Education Journal*, 33 (2005), p. 54.
9 *Ibid.*, p. 57.

10 *Ibid.*
11 P. D. Facci, 'On human potential: peace and conflict transformation fostered through dance' (Master's Dissertation, Universitat Innsbruck, 2011), p. 39.
12 T. Ney and E. Humber, 'Dance as metaphor: the metaphor of dance and peace building', in *The Choreography of Resolution*, ed. by M. LeBaron, C. MacLeod and A. F. Acland (Chicago: American Bar Association, Section of Dispute Resolution, 2013), p. 88.
13 Facci, 'On human potential'; L. J. Pruitt, *Youth Peacebuilding: Music, Gender, and Change* (Albany: State University of New York (SUNY) Press, 2013).
14 Swick, 'Preventing violence', p. 56.
15 Facci, 'On human potential', p. 117.
16 E. R. Jeffrey, 'Dance in peacebuilding: space, relationships, and embodied interactions' (PhD thesis, Queensland University of Technology, 2017).
17 R. J. Jagers *et al.*, 'Protective factors associated with preadolescent violence: preliminary work on a cultural model', *American Journal of Community Psychology*, 40 (2007), p. 138.
18 A. Joscelyne *et al.*, 'Mental health functioning in the human rights field: findings from an international Internet-based survey', *PLOS One*, 10 (2015), https://doi.org/10.1371/journal.pone.0145188; T. H. Holtz *et al.*, 'Mental health status of human rights workers, Kosovo, June 2000', *Journal of Traumatic Stress*, 15 (2002), p. 394.
19 Joscelyne *et al.*, 'Mental health functioning in the human rights field'; Holtz *et al.*, 'Mental health status of human rights workers', p. 395.
20 A. Cárdenas and N. Méndez, 'Self-care as a political strategy', *Sur International Journal on Human Rights*, 14 (2017), pp. 171–80; J. Barry and J. Djordjevic, *What's the Point of Revolution if We Can't Dance?* (Boulder: Urgent Action for Women's Human Rights, 2007).
21 Cárdenas and Méndez, 'Self-care as a political strategy'.
22 C. Irvine, 'Building emotional intelligence', in *The Choreography of Resolution*, ed. by M. LeBaron, C. MacLeod and A. F. Acland (Chicago: American Bar Association, Section of Dispute Resolution, 2013), p. 257.
23 N. Head, 'Tango: the intimate dance of conflict transformation', OpenDemocracy (22 August 2013), available at: www.opendemocracy.net/en/transformation/tango-intimate-dance-of-conflict-transformation/ (accessed 14 October 2019).
24 Facci, 'On human potential', p. 16.
25 N. Premaratna and R. Bleiker, 'Art and peacebuilding: how theatre transforms conflict in Sri Lanka', in *Palgrave Advances in Peacebuilding: Critical Developments and Approaches*, ed. by O. P. Richmond (Basingstoke: Palgrave Macmillan, 2010), pp. 376–91; L. J. Pruitt, *Youth peacebuilding (2013);* S. J. A. Mason, S. A. Nan and V. van de Loe, 'Dancing through conflict: developing intuition for mediation', in *The Choreography of Resolution*, ed.

by M. LeBaron, C. MacLeod and A. F. Acland (Chicago: American Bar Association, Section of Dispute Resolution, 2013), pp. 286–308.
26 M. Eddy, 'Dancing solutions to conflict: field-tested somatic dance for peace', *Journal of Dance Education*, 16 (2016), p. 103.
27 J. Siapno, 'Dance and martial arts in Timor Leste: the performance of resilience in a post-conflict environment', *Journal of Intercultural Studies*, 33 (2012), p. 428.
28 *Ibid.*, p. 429.
29 Beausoleil, 'Dance and neuroscience', p. 55.
30 *Ibid.*, p. 58.
31 Eddy, 'Dancing solutions to conflict', p. 104.
32 Facci, 'On human potential', p. 48.
33 Lederach, *The Moral Imagination*, p. 118.
34 Head, 'Tango'.
35 Beausoleil, 'Dance and neuroscience', p. 76.
36 P. Condon *et al.*, 'Meditation increases compassionate responses to suffering', *Psychological Science*, 24 (2013), p. 2126.
37 H. Berents, *Young People and Everyday Peace: Exclusion, Insecurity and Peacebuilding in Colombia* (New York and London: Routledge, 2018), p. 176.
38 Beausoleil, 'Dance and neuroscience', p. 59.
39 *Ibid.*, p. 78.
40 M. LeBaron and C. MacLeod, 'Introduction: let's dance', in *The Choreography of Resolution*, ed. by M. LeBaron, C. MacLeod and A. F. Acland (Chicago: American Bar Association, Section of Dispute Resolution, 2013), p. 46.
41 Beausoleil, 'Dance and neuroscience', p. 61.
42 L. B. Wilcox, *Bodies of Violence: Theorizing Embodied Subjects in International Relations* (Oxford: Oxford University Press, 2015).
43 Ney and Humber, 'Dance as metaphor', p. 100.
44 D. Davies, 'Dancing around the issues: prospects for an empirically grounded philosophy of dance', *Journal of Aesthetics and Art Criticism*, 71 (2013), pp. 195–202; S. Reed, 'The politics and poetics of dance', *Annual Review of Anthropology*, 27 (1998), p. 511.
45 Ney and Humber, 'Dance as metaphor', p. 83.
46 Beausoleil, 'Dance and neuroscience', p. 63.
47 *Ibid.*, p. 78.
48 *Ibid.*, p. 68.
49 Beausoleil and LeBaron, 'What moves us', p. 141.
50 Eddy, 'Dancing solutions to conflict', p. 99.
51 B. Ehrenreich, *Dancing in the Streets: A History of Collective Joy* (London: Granta Publications, 2007), p. 24.
52 Beausoleil and LeBaron, 'What moves us', p. 139.
53 *Ibid.*, p. 135.
54 *Ibid.*, p. 142.

55 LeBaron and MacLeod, 'Introduction', p. 42.
56 J. Parviainen, 'Choreographing resistances: spatial–kinaesthetic intelligence and bodily knowledge as political tools in activist work', *Mobilities*, 5 (2010), p. 311.
57 Wilcox, *Bodies of Violence*.
58 K. M. Teaiwa, 'Choreographing difference: the (body) politics of Banaban dance', *Contemporary Pacific*, 24 (2012), p. 67.
59 *Ibid.*, p. 66.
60 *Ibid.*, p. 84.
61 G. Hampshire, 'Saddle Lake dancer lands prestigious role in one of the world's largest powwows', CBC News (23 April 2017), available at: www.cbc.ca/news/canada/edmonton/indigenous-dancer-missing-murdered-alberta-1.4079501 (accessed 24 October 2019).
62 L. Beeston, 'Red dresses a visual reminder of missing, murdered indigenous women', *Star* [Toronto] (21 March 2017), available at: www.thestar.com/news/gta/2017/03/21/red-dresses-a-visual-reminder-of-missing-and-murdered-indigenous-women.html (accessed 24 October 2019).
63 Wilcox, *Bodies of Violence*.
64 *Ibid.*
65 L. Åhäll, 'The dance of militarisation: a feminist security studies take on "the political"', *Critical Studies on Security*, 4 (2016), p. 158.
66 *Ibid.*
67 *Ibid.*
68 *Ibid.*, pp. 152–7.
69 Ney and Humber, 'Dance as metaphor', p. 93.
70 LeBaron and MacLeod, 'Introduction', p. 53.
71 Beausoleil, 'Dance and neuroscience'.
72 *Ibid.*

Conclusion

Throughout this book, we have pursued our commitment to peace, arts and pluralism, and have explored the links between dance and peacebuilding. In particular, we have examined existing theories and approaches to peace and conflict through the lens of creative movement, which presents itself as a relevant way to engage with aesthetic politics. Drawing on our training and the existing evidence base in Peace and Conflict Studies, IR, Politics and Dance, we have taken a deep dive into practice as observed and experienced through the work of one global NGO working for peace through dance across three different countries – Colombia, the Philippines and the US. We observed and interviewed the young peer leaders in the programme across these diverse sites, and were able to situate our learning with nuance and draw out commonalities across difference.

Although traditionally IR and Peace and Conflict Studies are seen as central to investigating, preventing and redressing conflict, they have rarely engaged with dance and creative movement. Even during the course of writing this book, the visibility of dance as a means of embodying the political has continued to increase, while young peoples' voices are gaining strength in the pursuit of peace. We have benefitted greatly from those pioneering scholars and practitioners who have stretched their imaginations to engage with multiple senses and connect with bodies as political and capable

Conclusion

of social transformation, including through everyday practices of peace. We have drawn on their insights in our investigation of dance and peacebuilding.

Overall, our research leaves us confident that dance and creative movement can be effectively engaged in the creation of peace. Dance, as an embodied, aesthetic vehicle, can support relationships among diverse actors; enable the expression and embracing of emotions; add to the range of avenues to engage in dialogue; and traverse perceived boundaries between the local and global. In considering the process of how such changes may occur, we have witnessed challenges as well as prospects when it comes to peacebuilding and transforming conflict.

Creative movement and dance, like other means for peacebuilding, are subject to risks, including outcomes that may not best support sustainable peace. At the same time, due to its flexibility and ephemerality, dance resists the dominant tendency to focus on quantifiable, technical approaches to peacebuilding. While making it more challenging to measure, this intangibility provides a useful counterpoint to established narratives of building peace.

Dance can teach us how peace might be enacted and articulated, including through playing a part in broader transformative social movements for peace. In this study, we have worked with young peacebuilders across diverse communities locally and globally. In doing so, we have sought to shed light on ways that violence and conflict may be experienced and peace may be enacted and understood. Our investigation includes attention to how cultural or geographic differences and other factors, including but not limited to age and gender, may play an important role in what peace means and how it can be realised.

Retracing our steps: reflecting on the research

Around the world, dance and music are recognised as important to both cultural expression and social cohesion. We argue for recognising the ways dance can support a range of approaches to communication, assist in building relationships across difference and promote the participation of diverse actors in peacebuilding. To better understand these prospects, we shared a basic typology of six categories to understand efforts in dance-based peacebuilding – therapeutic; artist-led social change or protest; community-led social change or protest; collective forms; educational; and diplomatic (see Chapter 1). While acknowledging that these categories can coexist, blend and/or overlap, we suggest that considering a programme's intent and the category or categories into which it might fit are useful in further articulating the field of practice.

In our research we explored how working with youth across diverse sites illuminates the need for intersectional, plural approaches to understanding and practising peace. This builds on previous research identifying the importance and political significance of young people in peacebuilding. We also question why, despite international efforts, young people remain on the sidelines of peace initiatives and are not sufficiently recognised and engaged in policy or practice. Our research indicates that dance can be a meaningful, impactful pathway to support youth leadership for peace. The data gathered also points to the significance of ensuring peacebuilding efforts are flexible, age specific, gender sensitive and culturally relevant.

We investigated what dance can tell us about local and/or global approaches to peacebuilding, including how the two are defined and interact, and the political implications of this interchange. To consider this in practice, we looked closely at 'hub dance exchanges'. The hub dances were seen as a way to create cross-cultural exchange in the pursuit of peace. The hub dances prompt further examination of the different cultural contexts in which conflict occurs and the tensions between the possibilities of instilling stereotypes or being valued for difference. We also considered the ways in which the creation, practice and exchange of hub dances enacted meaning

Conclusion

around identity for self, others and the community, and how this relates to peacebuilding more broadly.

We then explored the concept of empathy, including the prospects and challenges it poses in arts-based peacebuilding. To do so, we analysed a set of creative dance activities involving the use of mirroring. A common dance activity, mirroring has been deployed in many settings and contexts, including use as an icebreaker in some mainstream peacebuilding resources. As seen in our three case studies, mirroring can invite interpersonal exchange and support the development of empathy. This empathy can promote understanding across difference and likewise contribute to peacebuilding, including the restructuring of relationships after violence. In short, we suggest that (1) nonviolent ways of expressing emotions are crucial for peacebuilding; (2) empathy is a key emotion to address in the aim of peacebuilding; and (3) dance activities, including mirroring, when used with critical reflection, can offer a promising way to foster empathy and thus support peacebuilding.

We noted how practitioner self-care has been underexplored in Peace and Conflict Studies, even though peacebuilders themselves could benefit immensely from further investigation in this area. We propose that dance has broader implications in peacebuilding because it can enable a more reflective stance for considering conflict. It has the potential to offer new and creative directions for pursuing peace. Our research suggests that through dance, participants had an opportunity to express a deeper sense of self-understanding, embodiment and strength to go on with the work of peace. In the midst of difficult work in circumstances of conflict, the peacebuilders we worked with appreciated opportunities that dance provided to relieve stress and re-engage with their bodies. Acknowledging that diverse bodies may be placed differently in settings of conflict, we also interrogated the prospects and challenges posed by gender and age norms in particular sites of peacebuilding.

Broader reflections on our research themes: choreographing next steps

As the global community continues to seek ways to build peace that are inclusive of people across differences – such as race, religion, gender, culture, age and locality – and that revise, supplement or replace existing dominant approaches, this book provides a valuable in-depth analysis that includes exploring the benefits and challenges of arts-based peacebuilding practice. In considering dance and peacebuilding, this book seeks to build the resources available for understanding sociopolitical and aesthetic effects at work in different communities with varying conflict dynamics.

This book incorporates multiple perspectives including elements of dance practice, participant voices and critical political analysis, and it reveals important implications and nuances regarding an arts-based peace initiative that, when applied, can offer needed understandings within the peacebuilding field. By exploring the politics of dancing peace, and the interpersonal interactions and ability to 'practise peace' as well as the local and global connections, this book highlights and analyses key themes in arts-based peacebuilding work. Key findings from this research include the ways in which dance is perceived as being useful in peacebuilding, the value of embodiment and practising peace with others, and the potential for dance to bridge perceived local–global divides.

Firstly, participant statements indicated 'that dance can be useful in engaging youth in peacebuilding but that it must be applied in sensitive, reflexive and culturally relevant ways to appeal to and include both young men and young women'.[1] Considering age is salient, given the importance of and growth in attention paid to the roles of youth in peace in conflict. The young participants in this project articulated the ways in which dance had been useful for peacebuilding. For example, they explained how dance served as a nonviolent means of communication and a way to connect with one's feelings in a peace education context. Dance was seen

Conclusion

as something that many young people could relate to, as it was culturally relevant and familiar, and it was also something that did not require a great deal of expensive equipment or training. Dance was also understood as a way to release and reduce stress, an important aspect of recovering from violence already witnessed or experienced.

Participants also pointed to a variety of limitations regarding what dance could do and how. In particular, they identified how short-term funding cycles, which are common across global peacebuilding initiatives, can at times create short-sighted programmes. They also noted that, without attention to access and inclusion, efforts to engage youth in dance and creative movement for peacebuilding might overlook the needs of some people – for example, people living with disabilities or those who speak a different language from the one deployed in the dance programmes. These limitations are not inherent to dance, nor are they always present, yet they should be given careful consideration across arts-based peacebuilding approaches nonetheless.

Through looking at young people's practice and understanding of dance and creative movement for peace, we can gain insights into local and global peacebuilding efforts, while noting how the two are understood, connect and may aid in creating one another. By listening to the young people involved in this research across the three case study sites, we learned of the ways in which they get involved in building cultures of peace locally, nationally, regionally and globally, despite so often being sidelined in formal political efforts at building peace.

Instead of accepting their exclusion, the young people we worked with explained how they envision peace, like violence, as occurring on a spectrum that crosses a number of scales. Many of them saw this as beginning with the self or the individual, expanding to the local community, and then more broadly to create and sustain global communities committed to peace. For young people in particular, this offered important connections they could use in building peace as well as opportunities for themselves in a connected world that often values international networks.

Research participants reported that they found dance and creative movement relevant for making these global connections for peace. While dance may not be a universal language, it is nonetheless commonly understood as a platform for sharing meaning, including across difference. Many participants also highlighted the need to better 'translate' programmes across cultures to ensure local relevance and respect for various cultural contexts.

Connecting with and expressing emotions is a vital aspect of peacebuilding. This emotional engagement can be accessed through empathy, and dance and creative movement facilitate that process. We have also highlighted limits and challenges to studying and practising empathy in the pursuit of peace, as well as how these challenges were addressed (or not) in the case studies. Through exploring these tensions, we have made a case for incorporating emotion in peacebuilding without sidelining the faculties of critical reasoning necessary for the pursuit of social justice – a key element of positive peace.

Lastly, the young peacebuilders involved in this research often referred to aspects of understanding and caring for the self as critical for peace, with many expressing the opinion that peace could only be possible or sustained if it started in or was present in the self. They explained that self-knowledge or awareness and self-esteem could be crucial for this process, as could the ability to feel relaxed or safe in one's own physical body. They also provided insights into the complex ways different bodies may be placed and understood in this context.

As young people around the world are increasingly taking up the work of peacebuilding, it is useful to reflect and share knowledge and approaches. The young peacebuilders we came to know provided insightful knowledge on how dance and creative movement expressed in physical and embodied ways can foster and sustain peacebuilding. In particular, self-care for peacebuilders has been underexplored,

Conclusion

and our research suggests that dance and creative movement can offer an important means for nurturing self-care for peacebuilders. This may occur through practices that enable individuals involved in peace efforts to deal with stress in healthy ways and find methods to relax, breathe and re-engage with their bodies so that they can access the strength, courage and stamina to continue their crucial work, including in conflict-affected and often overwhelming circumstances.

Overall, it appears that dance and creative movement, when applied in thoughtful ways, can help foster peacebuilding. This is not to say that dance cannot also be used ineffectively, sometimes even creating exclusions. However, when used well in the pursuit of peace, dance can have much to offer when it comes to seeking harmony within the dissonance of conflict.

While the research for this book has taught us a lot, as with any truly interesting and timely research area, it also poses a number of further questions. While it would be impossible to outline them all here, providing some potential future directions is worthwhile in aiming to stimulate further discussion and research in the pursuit of peace. Some key questions among the many that merit further exploration include:

- What are the long-term effects of dance-based peacebuilding initiatives?
- Are there differences in whether and how creative movement for peace might be encountered, experienced or adapted across different age groups beyond young people?
- Do different styles of music lead to different groups participating?
- What are best-practice efforts for better accounting for and including people with a wide range of mobility issues or other disabilities when conducting movement-based peacebuilding?
- How might the use of different dance styles or genres influence who takes part and what the outcomes of dance-based peace programmes might be?

- How can dance best be shared across different countries and cultures without creating or reinforcing existing stereotypes?
- What differences might arise between programmes where leaders choreograph movements compared to those where participants are also co-creators of the dance?
- How do experiences where participants generate their own creative material contribute to their peace work?
- How would the activities we describe in this book fare in settings with different contexts of conflict?
- Does it make a difference whether such programmes refer to their work as 'dance', 'creative movement' or another term?
- How might scholars, practitioners, policymakers and donors reimagine evaluation in peacebuilding to include and value more embodied and creative approaches?
- What practices might effectively support peacebuilder self-care?

Following insights from Roland Bleiker in his work on aesthetic politics, our investigation of dance and peacebuilding has not been aimed at being prescriptive, but rather has been conducted in the spirit of seeking to uncover new ways of 'sensing the political' in ways that allow our research to speak to a broad audience while eschewing all-encompassing explanations in favour of fostering self-reflexivity and pluralism.[2] As Bleiker explains, it is crucial that we open our hearts and minds to ideas and people that have been excluded, including in our pursuit of peace. While we will have surely failed at many points, we aspire to continue in our quest to be reflective and maintain an open mind in our search for new aesthetic ways to encounter and address ever-evolving political dilemmas.[3]

Keeping this overall goal in mind, and following the wisdom provided by 'Juan', one of our research participants in Colombia, we hope our readers can walk away challenged to ask questions, risk the vulnerability of creativity and move towards a more peaceful world. As such, we leave you with some of his words:

Conclusion

What's next? Leave them a little seed; somehow make them see a different world ... I think that there are ... things that move the world and that can be done by any person ... These are love, peace, willingness and courage.

May you search for and find them all in your daily dance of life.

Notes

1 L. J. Pruitt, 'Gendering the study of children and youth in peacebuilding', *Peacebuilding*, 3 (2015), pp. 157–70.
2 R. Bleiker, 'In search of thinking space: reflections on the aesthetic turn in international political theory', *Millennium: Journal of International Studies*, 45 (2017), pp. 258–64.
3 *Ibid.*, p. 264.

References

Abu-Nimer, M., 'Toward the theory and practice of positive approaches to peacebuilding', in *Positive Approaches to Peacebuilding: A Resource for Innovators*, ed. by C. Sampson, M. Abu-Nimer, C. Liebler and D. Whitney (Washington DC: PACT Publications, 2003), pp. 13–23.

Acarón, T., 'The practitioner's body of knowledge: dance/movement in training programmes that address violence, conflict and peace' (PhD thesis, University of Aberdeen, 2015).

Ackerly, B. A., M. Stern and J. True, 'Conclusion', in *Feminist Methodologies for International Relations*, ed. by B. A. Ackerly, M. Stern and J. True (Cambridge: Cambridge University Press, 2006), pp. 261–3.

Åhäll, L., 'The dance of militarisation: a feminist security studies take on "the political"', *Critical Studies on Security*, 4 (2016), pp. 154–68.

Aistrope, T., 'Popular culture, the body and world politics', *European Journal of International Relations*, 1 (2019), pp. 1–24.

Alexander, N., and M. LeBaron, 'Dancing to the rhythm of the role-play: applying dance intelligence to conflict resolution', *Hamline Journal of Public Law and Policy*, 33 (2012), pp. 327–62.

———, 'Building kinesthetic intelligence: dance in conflict-resolution education', in *The Choreography of Resolution*, ed. by M. LeBaron, C. MacLeod and A. F. Acland (Chicago: American Bar Association, Section of Dispute Resolution, 2013), pp. 220–56.

———, 'Embodied conflict resolution: resurrecting roleplay-based curricula through dance', in *Educating Negotiators for a Connected World*, ed. by C. Honeyman, J. Coben and A. Wei-Min Lee (Saint Paul: DRI Press, 2013), pp. 539–69.

Alford, C. F., 'Mirror neurons, psychoanalysis, and the age of empathy', *International Journal of Applied Psychoanalytic Studies*, 13 (2016), pp. 7–23.

Anderl, F., 'The myth of the local: how international organizations localize norms rhetorically', *Review of International Organizations*, 11 (2016), pp. 197–218.

References

Anderson, M. B., and L. Olson, *Confronting War: Critical Lessons for Peace Practitioners* (Cambridge, MA: The Collaborative for Development Action, 2003).

'A resolution recognizing the Alvin Ailey American Dance Theater for 50 years of service to the performing arts', S. Res. 490, 110th Congress (2008), available at: www.govtrack.us/congress/bills/110/sres490/text (accessed 9 May 2017).

Arslanian, S., 'How music and dance can nurture peace', *New Times* [Rwanda] (25 September 2015), available at: www.newtimes.co.rw/section/read/192883 (accessed 4 January 2018).

AUC, 'African youth charter' (Banjul: African Union Commission, 2006).

Avruch, K., *Culture and Conflict Resolution* (Washington DC: United States Institute of Peace Press, 1998).

Ayindo, B., 'Arts approaches to peace: playing our way to transcendence?', in *Peacebuilding in Traumatized Societies*, ed. by B. Hart (Boulder: University Press of America, 2008), pp. 185–204.

Baker, S., and B. M. Z. Cohen, 'From snuggling and snogging to sampling and scratching: girls' nonparticipation in community-based music activities', *Youth and Society*, 39 (2008), pp. 316–39.

Barry, J., and J. Djordjevic, *What's the Point of Revolution if We Can't Dance?* (Boulder: Urgent Action for Women's Human Rights, 2007).

Beausoleil, E., 'Dance and neuroscience: implications for conflict transformation', in *The Choreography of Resolution*, ed. by M. LeBaron, C. MacLeod and A. F. Acland (Chicago: American Bar Association, Section of Dispute Resolution, 2013), pp. 55–80.

Beausoleil, E., and M. LeBaron, 'What moves us: dance and neuroscience implications for conflict approaches', *Conflict Resolution Quarterly*, 31 (2013), pp. 133–58.

Beeston, L., 'Red dresses a visual reminder of missing, murdered indigenous women', *Star* [Toronto] (21 March 2017), available at: www.thestar.com/news/gta/2017/03/21/red-dresses-a-visual-reminder-of-missing-and-murdered-indigenous-women.html, accessed 24 October 2019.

Behrends, A., S. Müller and I. Dziobek, 'Moving in and out of synchrony: a concept for a new intervention fostering empathy through interactional movement and dance', *The Arts in Psychotherapy*, 39 (2012), pp. 107–16.

Benhabib, S., *The Claims of Culture: Equality and Diversity in the Global Era* (Princeton: Princeton University Press, 2002).

Berents, H., 'From the margins: conflict-affected young people, social exclusion, and an embodied everyday peace in Colombia' (PhD thesis, University of Queensland, 2013).

———, 'An embodied everyday peace in the midst of violence', *Peacebuilding*, 3 (2015), pp. 1–14.

———, *Young People and Everyday Peace: Exclusion, Insecurity and Peacebuilding in Colombia* (New York and London: Routledge, 2018).

References

Berents, H., and L. J. Pruitt, 'Not just victims or threats: young people win recognition as workers for peace', *The Conversation* (16 December 2015), available at: https://theconversation.com/not-just-victims-or-threats-young-people-win-recognition-as-workers-for-peace-52284 (accessed 18 October 2019).

Berrol, C., 'Neuroscience meets dance/movement therapy: mirror neurons, the therapeutic process and empathy', *The Arts in Psychotherapy*, 33 (2006), pp. 302–15.

Bierschenk, T., 'From the anthropology of development to the anthropology of global social engineering', *Zeitschrift für Ethnologie*, 139 (2014), pp. 73–98.

Björkdahl, A., and S. Buckley-Zistel, *Spatializing Peace and Conflict: Mapping the Production of Places, Sites and Scales of Violence* (London: Palgrave Macmillan, 2016).

Blanchet-Cohen, N., and L. Brunson, 'Creating settings for youth empowerment and leadership: an ecological perspective', *Child and Youth Services*, 35 (2014), pp. 216–36.

Bleiker, R., *Aesthetics and World Politics* (New York: Palgrave Macmillan, 2009).

———, 'In search of thinking space: reflections on the aesthetic turn in international political theory', *Millennium: Journal of International Studies*, 45 (2017), pp. 258–64.

Blumenfeld-Jones, D. S., 'Bodily-kinesthetic intelligence and the democratic ideal', in *Multiple Intelligences Reconsidered*, ed. by J. L. Kincheloe (New York: Peter Lang, 2004), pp. 119–31.

Boege, V., P. Rinck and T. Debiel, 'Local–international relations and the recalibration of peacebuilding interventions: insights from the "laboratory" of Bougainville and beyond', INEF report (Duisburg: Institute for Development and Peace, University of Duisburg-Essen, 2017).

Bond, K., 'Dance and quality of life', in *Encyclopaedia of Quality of Life and Well-being Research*, ed. by A. C. Michalos (Dordrecht: Springer, 2014), pp. 1419–24.

Borer, T. A., J. Darby and S. McEvoy-Levy, *Peacebuilding After Peace Accords: The Challenges of Violence, Truth, and Youth* (Notre Dame: University of Notre Dame Press, 2006).

Bouvier, V. M., ed., *Colombia: Building Peace in a Time of War* (Washington DC: United States Institute of Peace, 2009).

Bräuchler, B., 'Social engineering the local for peace', *Social Anthropology*, 25 (2017), pp. 437–53.

———, 'The cultural turn in peace research: prospects and challenges', *Peacebuilding*, 6 (2018), pp. 17–33, https://doi.org/10.1080/21647259.2017.1368158.

Bräuchler, B., and P. Naucke, 'Peacebuilding and conceptualisations of the local', *Social Anthropology*, 25 (2017), pp. 422–36.

References

Brocklehurst, H., *Who's Afraid of Children? Children, Conflict and International Relations* (London: Ashgate, 2006).

Brown, A., V. Boege, K. Clements and A. Nolan, 'Challenging statebuilding as peacebuilding: working with hybrid political orders to build peace', in *Palgrave Advances in Peacebuilding: Critical Developments and Approaches*, ed. by O. P. Richmond (Basingstoke: Palgrave Macmillan, 2010), pp. 99–115.

Brown, M., 'Sex, scale and the "new urban politics": HIV-prevention strategies from Yaletown, Vancouver', in *Mapping Desire: Geographies of Sexualities*, ed. by D. Bell and G. Valentine (London and New York: Routledge, 1995), pp. 245–63.

Bubant, N., 'Vernacular security: the politics of feeling safe in global, national and local worlds', *Security Dialogue*, 36 (2005), pp. 275–96.

Buck, R., N. Rowe and R. Martin, *Talking Dance: Contemporary Histories from the Southern Mediterranean* (London: I.B. Tauris, 2014).

Buckley-Zistel, S., 'Frictional spaces: transitional justice between the global and the local', in *Friction and Peacebuilding: Global and Local Encounters in Post-Conflict Societies*, ed. by A. Björkdahl, K. Höglund, G. Millar, W. Verkoren and J. van der Lijn (Abingdon: Routledge, 2016), pp. 17–31.

Bulanda, J. J., K. Szarzynski, D. Siler and K. Tyson McCrea, '"Keeping it real": an evaluation audit of five years of youth-led program evaluation', *Smith College Studies in Social Work*, 83 (2013), pp. 279–302.

Cagoco-Guiam, R., 'Mindanao: conflicting agendas, stumbling blocks, and prospects toward sustainable peace', in *Searching for Peace in Asia Pacific: An Overview of Conflict Prevention and Peacebuilding Activities*, ed. by A. Heijams, N. Simmonds and H. Van de Veen (Boulder: Lynne Rienner, 2004), pp. 483–504.

Cárdenas, A., and N. Méndez, 'Self-care as a political strategy', *Sur International Journal on Human Rights*, 14 (2017), pp. 171–80.

Chiao, J. Y., and V. A. Mathur, 'Intergroup empathy: how does race affect empathic neural responses?', *Current Biology*, 20 (2010), pp. R478–80.

Cho, S., K. W. Crenshaw and L. McCall, 'Toward a field of intersectionality studies: theory, applications, and praxis', *Signs: Journal of Women and Culture in Society*, 38 (2013), pp. 785–810.

Chou, M., J. P. Gagnon, C. Hartung and L. J. Pruitt, *Young People, Citizenship and Political Participation: Combatting Civic Deficit?* (Lanham: Rowman & Littlefield, 2017).

Coe, D., and J. Strachan, 'Writing dance: tensions in researching movement or aesthetic experiences', *International Journal of Qualitative Studies in Education*, 15 (2002), pp. 497–511.

Cohen, C., 'Arts and building peace: affirming the basics and envisioning the future', *Insights*, Summer (2015).

Cohen, C., R. G. Varea and P. O. Walker, eds, *Acting Together I: Performance and the Creative Transformation of Conflict* (New York: New Village Press, 2011).

References

Condon, P., G. Desbordes, W. B. Miller and D. DeSteno, 'Meditation increases compassionate responses to suffering', *Psychological Science*, 24 (2013), pp. 2125–7.

Connolly, J., W. Josephson, J. Schnoll, E. Simkins-Strong, D. Pepler, A. Macpherson, J. Weiser, M. Moran and D. Jiang, 'Evaluation of a youth-led program for preventing bullying, sexual harassment, and dating aggression in middle schools', *Journal of Early Adolescence*, 35 (2015), pp. 403–34.

Coulter, C., *Bush Wives and Girl Soldiers: Women's Lives through War and Peace in Sierra Leone* (Ithaca: Cornell University Press, 2009).

Cowan, G., and A. Aresenault, 'Moving from monologue to dialogue to collaboration: the three layers of public diplomacy', *Annals of the American Academy of Political and Social Science*, 616 (2008), pp. 10–30.

Cox, K. R., 'Spaces of dependence, spaces of engagement and the politics of scale, or: looking for local politics', *Political Geography*, 17 (1998), pp. 1–24.

'Crime and despair in Baltimore', *The Economist* (29 June 2017), available at: www.economist.com/news/united-states/21724399-america-gets-safer-marylands-biggest-city-does-not-crime-and-despair-baltimore (accessed 18 December 2017).

Croft, C., 'Dance returns to American cultural diplomacy: the U.S. State Department's Dance Residency program and its after effects', *Dance Research Journal*, 45 (2013), pp. 23–39.

Davies, D., 'Dancing around the issues: prospects for an empirically grounded philosophy of dance', *Journal of Aesthetics and Art Criticism*, 71 (2013), pp. 195–202.

Delaney, D., and H. Leitner, 'The political construction of scale', *Political Geography*, 16 (1997), pp. 93–7.

Delgado, M., and L. Staples, *Youth-Led Community Organizing: Theory and Action* (New York: Oxford University Press, 2008).

Dolan, C., 'Has patriarchy been stealing the feminists' clothes? Conflict-related sexual violence and UN Security Council resolutions', *IDS Bulletin*, 45 (2014), pp. 80–4.

Dunphy, K., M. Elton and A. Jordan, 'Exploring dance/movement therapy in post-conflict Timor-Leste', *American Journal of Dance Therapy*, 36 (2014), pp. 189–208.

Eddy, M., 'Dancing solutions to conflict: field-tested somatic dance for peace', *Journal of Dance Education*, 16 (2016), pp. 99–111.

Ehrenreich, B., *Dancing in the Streets: A History of Collective Joy* (London: Granta Publications, 2007).

Elhaway, S., 'Violent paths to peace? Rethinking the conflict-development nexus in Colombia', *Colombia Internacional*, 67 (2008), pp. 84–100.

Engle Merry, S., *Human Rights and Gender Violence: Translating International Law into Local Justice* (Chicago: University of Chicago Press, 2006).

References

Enloe, C., *Maneuvers: The International Politics of Militarizing Women's Lives* (Berkeley: University of California Press, 2000).

———, *The Curious Feminist: Searching for Women in a New Age of Empire* (Berkeley: University of California Press, 2004).

Facci, P. D., 'On human potential: peace and conflict transformation fostered through dance' (Master's dissertation, Universitat Innsbruck, 2011).

Ferrari, P. F., and G. Rizzolatti, 'Mirror neuron research: the past and the future', *Philosophical Transactions of the Royal Society B: Biological Sciences*, 369 (2014), https://doi.org/10.1098/rstb.2013.0169.

Finlay, K. A., and W. G. Stephan, 'Improving intergroup relations: the effects of empathy on racial attitudes', *Journal of Applied Social Psychology*, 30 (2000), pp. 1720–37.

Forcey, L. R., and I. M. Harris, *Peacebuilding for Adolescents: Strategies for Educators and Community Leaders* (New York: Peter Lang Publishing, 1999).

Ford, T., 'For Liberian youth, a creative outlet in krumping', *All Things Considered*, National Public Radio (17 September 2012), available at: www.npr.org/2012/09/17/161283651/for-liberian-youth-a-creative-outlet-in-krumping (accessed 14 October 2019).

Foreman, K., 'Dancing on the endangered list: aesthetics and politics of indigenous dance in the Philippines', in *Moving History/Dancing Cultures: A Dance History Reader*, ed. by A. Dils and A. Cooper Albright (Middletown: Wesleyan University Press, 2001), pp. 384–9.

Foster, S. L., 'Choreographies of protest', *Theatre Journal*, 55 (2003), pp. 395–412.

Freedberg, D., and V. Gallese, 'Motion, emotion and empathy in aesthetic experience', *Trends in Cognitive Sciences*, 11 (2007), pp. 197–202.

Freedman, L., 'Moon Jae-in's diplomatic dance towards peace with North Korea', *New Statesman* (26 September 2018), available at: www.newstatesman.com/world/asia/2018/09/moon-jae-s-diplomatic-dance-towards-peace-north-korea (accessed 14 October 2019).

Gallese, V., 'Mirror neurons, embodied simulation, and the neural basis of social identification', *Psychoanalytic Dialogues*, 19 (2009), pp. 519–36.

Gilbert, A. G., *Creative Dance for All Ages: A Conceptual Approach* (Reston: American Alliance for Health, Physical Education, Recreation and Dance, 1992).

Gonye, J., 'Mobilizing dance/traumatizing dance: Kongonya and the politics of Zimbabwe', *Dance Research Journal*, 45 (2013), pp. 64–79.

Grau, A., 'Dancing bodies, spaces/places and the senses: a cross-cultural investigation', *Journal of Dance and Somatic Practices*, 3 (2011), pp. 5–24.

———, 'Why people dance – evolution, sociality and dance', *Dance, Movement and Spiritualities*, 2 (2015), pp. 233–54.

Hampshire, G., 'Saddle Lake dancer lands prestigious role in one of the world's largest powwows', CBC News (23 April 2017), available at: www.cbc.ca/news/canada/edmonton/indigenous-dancer-missing-murdered-alberta-1.4079501 (accessed 24 October 2019).

References

Hanna, J. L., *To Dance is Human* (Chicago: University of Chicago Press, 1979).

———, 'Dance and the "Women's War"', *Dance Research Journal*, 14 (1981), pp. 25–8.

———, 'A nonverbal language for imagining and learning: dance education in K-12 curriculum', *Educational Research*, 37 (2008), pp. 491–506.

Hansen, L., 'The Little Mermaid's silent security dilemma and the absence of gender in the Copenhagen School', *Millennium: Journal of International Studies*, 29 (2000), pp. 285–306.

Harris, A., *Young People and Everyday Multiculturalism* (New York and London: Routledge, 2013).

Head, N., 'Tango: the intimate dance of conflict transformation', OpenDemocracy (22 August 2013), available at: www.opendemocracy.net/en/transformation/tango-intimate-dance-of-conflict-transformation/ (accessed 14 October 2019).

———, 'A politics of empathy: encounters with empathy in Israel and Palestine', *Review of International Studies*, 42 (2016), pp. 95–113.

Henrizi, A., 'Building peace in hybrid spaces: women's agency in Iraqi NGOs', *Peacebuilding*, 3 (2015), pp. 75–89.

Heydarian, R. J., 'Mindanao crisis: a city on fire', Al Jazeera (27 May 2017), available at: www.aljazeera.com/indepth/opinion/2017/05/philippines-marital-law-rekindling-horrific-memories-170526131438289.html (accessed 18 December 2017).

Holmes, M., 'The force of face-to-face diplomacy: mirror neurons and the problem of intentions', *International Organization*, 67 (2013), pp. 829–61.

Holtz, T. H., P. Salama, B. L. Cardozo and C. A. Gotway, 'Mental health status of human rights workers, Kosovo, June 2000', *Journal of Traumatic Stress*, 15 (2002), pp. 389–95.

Hutchison, E., *Affective Communities in World Politics: Collective Emotions after Trauma* (Cambridge: Cambridge University Press, 2016).

Huynh, K., B. d'Costa and K. Lee-Koo, *Children and Global Conflict* (Cambridge: Cambridge University Press, 2015).

Irvine, C., 'Building emotional intelligence', in *The Choreography of Resolution*, ed. by M. LeBaron, C. MacLeod and A. F. Acland (Chicago: American Bar Association, Section of Dispute Resolution, 2013), pp. 257–85.

Isacson, A., and J. R. Rodriguez, 'Origins, evolution, and lessons of the Colombian peace movement', in *Colombia: Building Peace in a Time of War*, ed. by V. M. Bouvier (Washington DC: United States Institute of Peace, 2009).

Jabri, V., *War and the Transformation of Global Politics* (London: Palgrave, 2007).

Jackson, N., and T. Shapiro-Phim, eds, *Dance, Human Rights, and Social Justice: Dignity in Motion* (Lanham: Scarecrow Press (now Rowman & Littlefield), 2008).

References

Jagers, R. J., K. Sydnor, M. Mouttapa and B. R. Flay, 'Protective factors associated with preadolescent violence: preliminary work on a cultural model', *American Journal of Community Psychology*, 40 (2007), pp. 138–45.

Jeffrey, E. R., 'Dance in peacebuilding: space, relationships, and embodied interactions' (PhD thesis, Queensland University of Technology, 2017).

Jeffrey, E. R., and L. J. Pruitt, 'Dancing it out: building positive peace', in *Dance and the Quality of Life*, ed. by K. Bond (New York: Springer, 2018), pp. 475–93.

Jeong, H. W., *Peace and Conflict Studies: An Introduction* (Aldershot: Ashgate Publishing, 2000).

———, *Peacebuilding in Postconflict Societies: Strategy and Process* (Boulder: Lynne Rienner, 2005).

Johnson, H., 'Narrating entanglements: rethinking the local/global divide in ethnographic migration research', *International Political Sociology*, 10 (2016), pp. 383–97.

Jolliffe, D., and D. P. Farrington, 'Examining the relationship between low empathy and bullying', *Aggressive Behavior*, 32 (2006), pp. 540–50.

Joscelyne, A., S. Knuckey, M. L. Satterthwaite, R. A. Bryant, M. Li, M. Qian and A. D. Brown, 'mental health functioning in the human rights field: findings from an international Internet-based survey', *PLOS One*, 10 (2015), https://doi.org/10.1371/journal.pone.0145188.

J. R. A., 'Why Colombia's peace deal is taking so long to implement', *The Economist* (19 June 2017), available at: www.economist.com/blogs/economist-explains/2017/06/economist-explains-18 (accessed 18 December 2017).

Kappler, S., *Local Agency and Peacebuilding* (Basingstoke: Palgrave Macmillan, 2014).

Kilner, J., and R. Lemon, 'What we know currently about mirror neurons', *Current Biology*, 23 (2013), pp. R1057–62.

Koshland, L., J. Wilson and B. Wittaker, 'PEACE through dance/movement: evaluating a violence prevention program', *American Journal of Dance Therapy*, 26 (2004), pp. 69–90.

Krauss, N., *Forest Dark* (London: Bloomsbury, 2017).

Laban, R., *Laban's Principles of Dance and Movement Notation* (London: Macdonald & Evans, 1975).

Lamm, C., and J. Majdandzic, 'The role of shared neural activations, mirror neurons, a morality in empathy – a critical comment', *Neuroscience Research*, 90 (2015), pp. 14–24.

Lamotte, D., *World Changing 101: Challenging the Myth of Powerlessness* (Black Mountain: Dryad Publishing, 2014).

LeBaron, M., and C. MacLeod, 'Introduction: let's dance', in *The Choreography of Resolution*, ed. by M. LeBaron, C. MacLeod and A. F. Acland

References

(Chicago: American Bar Association, Section of Dispute Resolution, 2013), pp. 37–52.

LeBaron, M., C. MacLeod and A. F. Acland, eds, *The Choreography of Resolution: Conflict, Movement, and Neuroscience* (Chicago: American Bar Association, Section of Dispute Resolution, 2013).

Lederach, J. P., *Building Peace: Sustainable Reconciliation in Divided Societies* (Washington DC: United States Institute of Peace, 1997).

———, *The Moral Imagination: The Art and Soul of Building Peace* (Oxford: Oxford University Press, 2005).

Lee-Koo, K., 'Horror and hope: (re)presenting militarised children in global North–South relations', *Third World Quarterly*, 32 (2011), pp. 725–42.

Lopez Montaño, C., and A. Garciá Durán, 'The hidden costs of peace in Colombia', in *Colombia: Essays on Conflict, Peace, and Development*, ed. by A. Solimano (Washington DC: The World Bank, 2000), pp. 78–158.

Mac Ginty, R., 'Where is the local? Critical localism and peacebuilding', *Third World Quarterly*, 36 (2015), pp. 840–56.

Mac Ginty, R., and O. P. Richmond, 'The local turn in peace building: a critical agenda for peace', *Third World Quarterly*, 43 (2013), pp. 763–83.

MacLeod, C., 'Conclusion: new choreographies of conflict', in *The Choreography of Resolution*, ed. by M. LeBaron, C. MacLeod and A. F. Acland (Chicago: American Bar Association, Section of Dispute Resolution, 2013), pp. 552–57.

Marriage, Z., 'Evading biopolitical control: capoeira as total resistance', *Global Security*, 32 (2018), pp. 263–80.

Marston, S., 'The social construction of scale', *Progress in Human Geography*, 24 (2000), pp. 219–42.

Marx, M., and A. Delport, '"I am because we are" dancing for social change!', *Educational Research for Social Change*, 6 (2017), pp. 56–71.

Mason, S. J. A., S. A. Nan and V. van de Loe, 'Dancing through conflict: developing intuition for mediation', in *The Choreography of Resolution*, ed. by M. LeBaron, C. MacLeod and A. F. Acland (Chicago: American Bar Association, Section of Dispute Resolution, 2013), pp. 286–308.

May, R., 'The Philippines: the ongoing saga of Moro separatism', in *Diminishing Conflicts in Asia and the Pacific: Why Some Subside and Others Don't*, ed. by E. Aspinall, R. Jeffrey and A. J. Regan (Abingdon and New York: Routledge, Taylor & Francis Group, 2013), pp. 221–34.

McCormack, D. P., 'Geographies for moving bodies: thinking, dancing, spaces', *Geography Compass*, 2 (2008), pp. 1822–36.

McEvoy-Levy, S., 'Youth as social and political agents: issues in post-settlement peace building', Kroc Institute Occasional Paper #21:OP:2 (Notre Dame: Kroc Institute's Research Initiative on the Resolution of Ethnic Conflict, 2001).

References

——, 'Children, youth and peacebuilding', in *Critical Issues in Peace and Conflict Studies: Theory, Practice and Pedagogy*, ed. by T. Matyok, J. Senehi and S. Byrne (Lanham: Lexington Books, 2011), pp. 159–74.

McGarry, L. M., and F. A. Russo, 'Mirroring in dance/movement therapy: potential mechanisms behind empathy enhancement', *The Arts in Psychotherapy*, 38 (2011), pp. 178–84.

McIntyre, A., and T. Thusi, 'Children and youth in Sierra Leone's peacebuilding process', *African Security Review*, 12 (2003), https://doi.org/10.1080/10246029.2003.9627222.

Medcalf, R., 'Asia's "cold peace": China and India's delicate diplomatic dance', Brookings (24 September 2014), available at: www.brookings.edu/opinions/asias-cold-peace-china-and-indias-delicate-diplomatic-dance (accessed 4 January 2018).

Miels, E., 'Performing for peace: youth event to showcase music, dance, poetry, art', *Leader-Telegram* (30 April 2015), available at: www.leadertelegram.com/Entertainment/local-entertainment/2015/04/30/Performing-for-peace.html (accessed 4 January 2018).

Mies, M., *Patriarchy and Accumulation on a World Scale: Women in the Division of Labour* (London: Zed Books, 2014).

Mills, D., *Dance and Politics: Moving Beyond Boundaries* (Manchester: Manchester University Press, 2017).

——, 'Dancing the ruptured body: One Billion Rising, dance and gendered violence', in *Dance and Politics: Moving Beyond Boundaries* (Manchester: Manchester University Press, 2017), pp. 83–98.

Monbiot, G., *Out of the Wreckage: A New Politics for an Age of Crisis* (London and New York: Verso, 2017).

Montiel, C. J., R. B. Rodil and J. M. de Guzman, 'The Moro struggle and the challenge to peace building in Mindanao, Southern Philippines', in *Handbook of Ethnic Conflict*, ed. by D. Landis and R. D. Albert (New York: Springer, 2012), pp. 71–89.

Morris, G., and J. R. Giersdorf, eds, *Choreographies of 21st Century Wars* (Oxford: Oxford University Press, 2015).

Mortensen, J., 'An empirical investigation of an emerging youth-driven model of leadership: the Collective Change Youth Leadership Framework' (PhD thesis, Michigan State University, 2016).

Mortensen, J., L. Lichty, P. Foster-Fishman, S. Harfst, S. Hockin, K. Warsinske and K. Abdullah, 'Leadership through a youth lens: understanding youth conceptualizations of leadership', *Journal of Community Psychology*, 42 (2014), pp. 447–62.

Mouffe, C., *Agonistics: Thinking the World Politically* (London and New York: Verso, 2013).

Murray Brown, J., 'Complex dance to save the peace agreement', *Financial Times*, US edn (24 October 2001).

References

Neveu Kringelbach, H., 'Moving shadows of Casamance: performance and regionalism in Senegal', in *Dancing Cultures: Globalization, Tourism and Identity in the Anthropology of Dance*, ed. by H. Neveu Kringelbach and J. Skinner (New York and Oxford: Berghahn Books, 2012), pp. 143–60.

Ney, T., and E. Humber, 'Dance as metaphor: the metaphor of dance and peace building', in *The Choreography of Resolution*, ed. by M. LeBaron, C. MacLeod and A. F. Acland (Chicago: American Bar Association, Section of Dispute Resolution, 2013), pp. 81–108.

Office of the Secretary-General's Envoy on Youth, '#YouthStats: armed conflict' (New York: United Nations, 2016).

Özerdem, A., S. Podder and E. L. Quitoriano, 'Identity, ideology and child soldiering: community and youth participation in civil conflict – a study on the Moro Islamic Liberation Front in Mindanao, Philippines', *Civil Wars*, 12 (2010), pp. 304–25.

Paffenholz, T., 'Unpacking the local turn in peacebuilding: a critical assessment towards an agenda for future research', *Third World Quarterly*, 36 (2015), pp. 857–74.

Paris, R., 'Peacebuilding and the limits of liberal internationalism', *International Security*, 22 (1997), pp. 54–89.

Parviainen, J., 'Choreographing resistances: spatial–kinaesthetic intelligence and bodily knowledge as political tools in activist work', *Mobilities*, 5 (2010), pp. 311–29.

Pedwell, C., 'Affective (self-) transformations: empathy, neoliberalism and international development', *Feminist Theory*, 13 (2012), pp. 163–79.

Plancke, C., 'Dance performances in post-genocide Rwanda: remaking identity, reconnecting present and past', *Journal of Eastern African Studies*, 11 (2017), pp. 329–46.

Porter, E., 'Women, political decision-making, and peace-building', *Global Change, Peace and Security*, 15 (2003), pp. 245–62.

Premaratna, N., and R. Bleiker, 'Art and peacebuilding: how theatre transforms conflict in Sri Lanka', in *Palgrave Advances in Peacebuilding: Critical Developments and Approaches*, ed. by O. P. Richmond (Basingstoke: Palgrave Macmillan, 2010), pp. 376–91.

Pruitt, L. J., 'They drop beats, not bombs: a brief discussion of issues surrounding the potential of music and dance in youth peace-building', *Australian Journal of Peace Studies*, 3 (2008), pp. 10–28.

———, 'Creating a musical dialogue for peace', *International Journal of Peace Studies*, 16 (2011), pp. 81–103.

———, 'Music, youth and peacebuilding in Northern Ireland', *Global Change, Peace and Security*, 23 (2011), pp. 207–22.

———, '"Fixing the girls": neoliberal discourse and girls' participation in peacebuilding', *International Feminist Journal of Politics*, 15 (2013), pp. 58–76.

References

———, *Youth Peacebuilding: Music, Gender, and Change* (Albany: State University of New York (SUNY) Press, 2013).

———, 'The women, peace and security agenda: Australia and the agency of girls', *Australian Journal of Political Science*, 49 (2014), pp. 486–98.

———, 'Gendering the study of children and youth in peacebuilding', *Peacebuilding*, 3 (2015), pp. 157–70.

———, 'Youth leadership: an annotated bibliography' (London: PLAN International, 2017).

———, 'Global youth and peacebuilding', in *Handbook of Peace and Conflict Studies*, ed. by S. Byrne, T. Matyok and I. Scott (New York: Routledge, 2019).

Pruitt, L., H. Berents and G. Munro, 'Gender and age in the construction of male youth in the European "migration crisis"', *Signs: Journal of Women and Culture in Society*, 43 (2018), pp. 687–709.

Rai, S. M., 'Political performance: a framework for analysing democratic politics', *Political Studies*, 63 (2014), pp. 1179–97.

Ramsbotham, O., 'Conflict resolution in art and popular culture', in *Contemporary Conflict Resolution*, ed. by O. Ramsbotham, H. Miall and T. Woodhouse (Cambridge: Polity, 2011), pp. 347–58.

Reason, M., and D. Reynolds, 'Kinesthesia, empathy, and related pleasures: an inquiry into audience experiences of watching dance', *Dance Research Journal*, 42 (2010), pp. 49–75.

Reed, S., 'The politics and poetics of dance', *Annual Review of Anthropology*, 27 (1998), pp. 503–32.

Reedy, P., *Body, Mind and Spirit in Action* (Berkeley: Luna Dance Institute, 2015).

Richmond, O. P., 'Reclaiming peace in International Relations', *Millennium: Journal of International Studies*, 36 (2008), pp. 439–70.

———, 'A genealogy of peace and conflict theory', in *Palgrave Advances in Peacebuilding: Critical Developments and Approaches*, ed. by O. P. Richmond (Basingstoke: Palgrave Macmillan, 2010), pp. 14–38.

Rizzolatti, G., and L. Craighero, 'The mirror-neuron system', *Annual Review of Neuroscience*, 27 (2004), pp. 169–92.

Rizzolatti, G., L. Fadiga, V. Gallese and L. Fogassi, 'Premotor cortex and the recognition of motor actions', *Cognitive Brain Research*, 3 (1996), pp. 131–41.

Rowe, N., 'Dance education in the Occupied Palestinian Territories: hegemony, counter-hegemony and anti-hegemony', *Research in Dance Education*, 9 (2008), pp. 3–20.

———, 'Movement politics: dance criticism in the Occupied Palestinian Territories', *Forum for Modern Language Studies*, 46 (2010), pp. 441–59.

———, 'Dance and political credibility: the appropriation of Dabkeh by Zionism, Pan-Arabism, and Palestinian Nationalism', *Middle East Journal*, 65 (2011), pp. 363–80.

References

Sams, D. P., and S. D. Truscott, 'Empathy, exposure to community violence, and use of violence among urban, at-risk adolescents', *Child and Youth Care Forum*, 33 (2004), pp. 33–50.

Sanford, V., 'Peacebuilding in a war zone: the case of Colombian Peace Communities', *International Peacekeeping*, 10 (2003), pp. 107–18.

Schirch, L., *Ritual and Symbol in Peacebuilding* (Bloomfield: Kumarian Press, 2005).

Schulz, P., 'The "ethical loneliness" of male sexual violence survivors in Northern Uganda: gendered reflections on silencing', *International Feminist Journal of Politics*, 20 (2018), pp. 583–601.

Schwartz, S., *Youth and Post-Conflict Reconstruction: Agents of Change* (Washington DC: United States Institute of Peace Press, 2010).

Sengupta, S., 'For U.N. chief, a dance of diplomacy is halted by a misstep', *New York Times* (22 January 2014), available at: www.nytimes.com/2014/01/22/world/middleeast/for-un-chief-a-dance-of-diplomacy-is-halted-by-a-misstep.html?_r=0 (accessed 4 January 2018).

Shank, M., and L. Schirch, 'Strategic arts-based peacebuilding', *Peace and Change*, 33 (2008), pp. 217–42.

Siapno, J., 'Dance and martial arts in Timor Leste: the performance of resilience in a post-conflict environment', *Journal of Intercultural Studies*, 33 (2012), 427–43.

Sklar, D., 'Five premises for a culturally sensitive approach to dance', in *Moving History/Dancing Cultures: A Dance History Reader*, ed. by A. Dils and A. Cooper Albright (Middletown: Wesleyan University Press, 2001), pp. 30–32.

Smith, N., 'Contours of a spatialized politics: homeless vehicles and the production of geographical scale', *Social Text*, 33 (1992), pp. 54–81.

Sommers, M., 'Fearing Arica's young men: male youth, conflict, urbanization, and the case of Rwanda', in *The Other Half of Gender: Men's Issues in Development*, ed. by I. Bannon and M. Correia (Washington DC: The World Bank, 2006), pp. 137–58.

Staeheli, L., 'Empowering political struggle: spaces and scales of resistance', *Political Geography Compass*, 13 (1994), pp. 387–91.

Steele, J., 'Dancing with the enemy: they should hate each other, but a group of Sri Lankans have found peace through dance', *Guardian* (3 May 2001), available at: www.theguardian.com/culture/2001/may/03/artsfeatures1 (accessed 14 October 2019).

Stephan, W. G., and K. A. Finlay, 'The role of empathy in improving intergroup relations', *Journal of Social Issues*, 55 (1999), pp. 729–43.

Stinson, S., *Dance for Young Children: Finding the Magic in Movement* (Washington DC: American Alliance for Health and Physical Education, 1988).

Stock, C., 'Myth of a universal dance language: tensions between globalisation and cultural difference', in *Asia Pacific Dance Bridge: Academic Conference, Papers and Abstracts*, ed. by S. Burridge (Singapore: World Dance Alliance, 2001), pp. 246–62.

References

Sukarieh, M., and S. Tannock, *Youth Rising? The Politics of Youth in the Global Economy* (New York and London: Routledge, 2015).

Suliman, S., 'Mobility and the kinetic politics of migration and development', *Review of International Studies*, 42 (2016), pp. 702–23.

Swick, K., 'Preventing violence through empathy development in families', *Early Childhood Education Journal*, 33 (2005), pp. 53–59.

Swyngedouw, E., 'Neither global nor local: glocalization and the politics of scale', in *Spaces of Globalization: Reasserting the Power of the Local*, ed. by K. Cox (New York: Guilford, 1997), pp. 137–66.

Sylvester, C., 'Empathetic cooperation: a feminist method for IR', *Millennium: Journal of International Studies*, 23 (1993), pp. 315–34.

Teaiwa, K. M., 'Choreographing difference: the (body) politics of Banaban dance', *Contemporary Pacific*, 24 (2012), pp. 65–94.

Tickner, J. A., *Gender in International Relations: Feminist Perspectives on Achieving Global Security* (New York: Columbia University Press, 1992).

———, *Gendering World Politics: Issues and Approaches in the Post-Cold War Era* (New York: Columbia University Press, 2001).

UNDP, 'Youth strategy 2014–2017: empowered youth, sustainable future' (New York: United Nations Development Programme, 2014).

Ungerleider, J., 'Structured youth dialogue to empower peacebuilding and leadership', *Conflict Resolution Quarterly*, 29 (2012), pp. 381–402.

United Nations, 'UN Charter' (San Francisco: United Nations, 1945), full text available at: www.un.org/en/sections/un-charter/un-charter-full-text/ (accessed 18 October 2019).

US Agency for International Development, 'Sri Lankan youth celebrate International Day of Peace through song, dance and sport', ReliefWeb (26 September 2012), available at: https://reliefweb.int/report/sri-lanka/sri-lankan-youth-celebrate-international-day-peace-through-song-dance-and-sport (accessed 14 October 2019).

Verhovek, S. H., 'Rwandans share peace and unity through dance', *New York Times* (26 May 2000), available at www.nytimes.com/2000/05/26/us/purdy-journal-rwandans-share-peace-and-unity-through-dance.html (accessed 14 October 2019).

Watchlist on Children and Armed Conflict, 'No one to trust: children and armed conflict in Colombia' (New York: Watchlist on Children and Armed Conflict, 2012).

Watson, A. M. S., 'Can there be a "Kindered" peace?', *Ethics and International Affairs*, 22 (2008), pp. 35–42.

Wessel, K., 'DanceMotion USA: dance diplomacy for the 21st century', *Dance Informa* (2 February 2016), available at: www.danceinforma.com/2016/02/02/dancemotion-usa-dance-diplomacy-for-the-21st-century/ (accessed 23 February 2018).

References

'Western Michigan University student uses dance to promote peace in Iraq', *WMU News* (16 April 2010), available at: www.wmich.edu/wmu/news/2010/04/060.shtml (accessed 14 October 2019).

Wibben, A. T. R., 'Introduction: feminists study war', in *Researching War: Feminist Methods, Ethics and Politics*, ed. by A. T. R. Wibben (Abingdon and New York: Routledge, 2016), pp. 21–31.

Wilcox, L. B., *Bodies of Violence: Theorizing Embodied Subjects in International Relations* (Oxford: Oxford University Press, 2015).

Williams, F. C., 'The embodiment of social dynamics: a phenomenon of Western pop dance within a Filipino prison', *Research in Dance Education*, 14 (2013), pp. 39–56.

Zelizer, C., 'The role of artistic processes in peace-building in Bosnia-Herzegovina', *Peace and Conflict Studies*, 10 (2003), pp. 62–75.

Zelizer, C., and R. A. Rubinstein, eds, *Building Peace: Practical Reflections from the Field* (Sterling: Kumarian Press, 2009).

Index

aesthetic 1, 3, 5, 6, 26, 87, 92–4, 164–5, 168, 172
Alexander, Nadia 117, 128, 130
Anderl, Felix 79
Anderson, Mary B. 81
Avruch, Kevin 81
Ayindo, Babu 21

Baltimore 7, 9, 12, 36–7, 75
Beausoleil, Emily 117, 130, 143, 148
Behrends, Andrea 129
Benhabib, Seyla 83
Berents, Helen 151
Bleiker, Roland 92, 172
Bogotá 32, 52, 75
boys 47, 51, 53–65, 66, 68, 152
  see also gender; girls
Bräuchler, Birgit 81–3
Buckley-Zistel, Susanne 81

choreography 2, 8, 12, 27–8, 64, 78, 130
Christian 33–4, 96, 123
  see also religion
Coe, Dorothy 6
Colombia 2, 4, 7–9, 12, 31–5, 49, 50, 52, 54–7, 59–60, 63–4, 69, 83, 86–90, 92, 101, 115, 124, 133–4, 164, 172

community dance 7, 14, 112
conflict
  prevention 3
  resolution 3, 23–6, 32, 82, 96, 121, 134
  transformation 4, 24, 134, 146, 148, 154, 156
cooperation 46, 121
creative movement 8, 9, 11–12, 30, 35, 37, 45, 46, 75–6, 92–3, 104, 112, 114, 117, 122–3, 128, 129, 135, 142, 148–150, 152, 156, 160, 164–5, 169–72
cultural context 14, 76, 98, 105–6, 125, 166, 170
culture
  acquisition of 6
  as a characteristic 10, 15, 22, 26, 30, 33, 35, 57, 81–4, 86–7, 90–9, 104–5, 123–4, 126–7, 154, 168, 170, 172
  building of 76, 84, 106, 117, 143, 156, 169
  expression of 13, 20
  practice of 102
  and prejudice 34, 129

189

Index

dance
  Banaban 155–6
  hip hop 93
  hub dance(s) 14, 76–7, 94–100, 104–6, 166
  krumping 29–30
  Powwow, Gathering of Nations 156
  warm-up 8
dance therapy 14, 112
Dance Therapy Association, American 25
diplomacy 22, 27–8, 30, 129
disabilities
  and bullying 35
  and needs 11–12, 91, 133, 157, 169, 171
  and storytelling 29
Dziobek, Isabel 129

Eddy, Martha 25, 96, 147, 149
education 3, 14, 25, 26, 29, 32–6, 44, 53, 68, 112, 120, 154, 168
  peace 20, 103, 117, 135, 154
Ehrenreich, Barbara 114
elicitive peacebuilding 93
embodiment 3, 4, 8, 11, 13, 15, 20, 22–3, 25, 29, 93, 96, 113–14, 117, 128–30, 142, 144–5, 147, 151–2, 156, 167–8, 170
  bodies 3, 22–3, 25, 77, 114, 130, 133, 142, 144, 151, 154–9, 167
  emotions 3–4, 8, 25, 29, 58, 97, 111–23, 128, 130–1, 135, 150–1, 165, 167, 170
  empathy 8, 13–15, 20, 24, 36, 111–36, 143–4, 146, 150–1, 167, 170
  and prejudice 121, 124
Enloe, Cynthia 93
Ensler, Eve 2
  see also One Billion Rising

everyday peace 3, 5, 19, 46–7, 53, 151, 156, 165

Facci, Paula Ditzel 144, 146, 149
Farrington, David P. 118, 120
feminist 4, 47, 59, 124, 145, 152, 155–7
Finlay, Krystina A. 118, 124, 126

gender 10, 14–15, 45, 51–4, 56–66, 68, 70, 87, 125, 142, 152, 157–8, 165, 166–8
  see also boys; girls
girls 2, 47, 51, 53–67 *passim*, 152, 157
  see also boys; gender
global
  awareness 2, 4, 10–11, 20, 70, 93, 104, 124, 165
  movements 2, 126
  NGOs 7–9, 68, 101, 164
  peacebuilding 3, 4, 11, 13–14, 23, 29, 31, 48, 75–106, 164–6, 168–70
  politics 4, 23, 25, 93, 157
  significance 3
Grau, Andrée 6, 114

Hanna, Judith Lynne 6
Harris, Anita 84
Head, Naomi 24, 118–19, 125–6
Holmes, Marcus 129
homogenisation 14, 77
hub dance see *dance, hub dance(s)*
hybridity, concept of 79, 93

identity 24, 46, 51–2, 57, 77, 82, 90, 93, 104, 123, 152, 155–6, 167
injustice 61, 121, 124, 143
International Relations (IR), study of 1, 3–4, 13, 19, 23, 47, 78, 119, 129, 155–6, 164
international relations 46
Irvine, Charlie 146

Index

Jolliffe, Darrick 118, 120
justice 24, 45, 121, 124, 141
  see also injustice; social justice

kinaesthetic
  communication 128
  empathy 15, 130

Lamotte, David 1
Latin America 86, 88
LeBaron, Michelle 117, 128, 130, 154
Lederach, John Paul 5, 19–21, 75, 81, 142, 150
local
  concerns 23
  conflict 4
  cultural context 31, 55, 57, 77, 82–4, 102, 105
  forms 20
  global interaction 2, 11, 79, 84, 92–4, 102, 147, 165, 168
  peacebuilding 3, 4, 10, 13–14, 31–2, 48, 75–106, 119, 165–6, 168–70
  performance 2, 26, 29, 31, 37, 95–7
  politics 79–80
Lumad 33, 124

McEvoy-Levy, Siobhán 84–7
Mac Ginty, Roger 81
Mies, Maria 52
Mindanao 7, 33–5, 96, 102, 111, 126
mirroring 14–15, 111–12, 128–36, 167
Moro 33–4, 123
  see also Muslim
Mouffe, Chantal 113–14
Müller, Sybille 129
music 6, 13, 20–1, 29, 33, 37, 44, 61, 96, 99, 114, 116, 130, 165, 171
Muslim 33–5, 96–7, 123–4, 133

neurons 128–30
  mirror 128–9
neuroscience 1, 19, 128
New York City 7, 9, 36, 75
nonverbal 6, 113, 120, 126, 128, 154

Olson, Lara 81
One Billion Rising (OBR) 2

Paris, Roland 80
Parviainen, Janna 155
Peace and Conflict Studies 1, 4, 13, 15, 19, 82, 142, 155, 164, 167
Pedwell, Carolyn 118, 125–7
peer leader(ship) 8–9, 44–5, 61, 66–70, 88, 92, 94–5, 101, 116, 164
Philippines 2, 4, 7–9, 30–1, 33–5, 50, 54, 60, 62, 75, 89–90, 92, 95–7, 101–2, 111, 115–16, 122, 125–6, 131, 146, 164
Plancke, Carine 94
positive peace 7, 20, 24, 47, 62, 112, 121, 127, 136, 170
post-conflict 3, 7, 25, 147
protest 20, 25–6, 166

reconciliation 4, 14, 21, 23, 29, 81, 113, 126
relational approaches 21, 24, 27, 77, 93, 96, 114, 141, 143–4, 158
religion 10, 30, 123–4, 133, 168
  see also Christian; Lumad; Moro; Muslim
Richmond, Oliver 61, 81–2

Sams, Deanna Palmeri 118, 120
scale(s)
  concepts of 84–5, 92, 94, 100–1, 103–4
  of peacebuilding action 77–80, 85, 88, 105, 169
  utility of 103

Index

Schirch, Lisa 21, 93
schools 8, 32, 37, 73, 85–6, 95, 101, 103, 147, 153
self-care 15, 24, 127, 141–2, 145–60 *passim*, 167, 170–2
self-esteem 120, 127, 142, 144–5, 147, 159, 170
Shank, Michael 21, 93
Siapno, Jacqueline 24, 147
Smith, Neil 77
social
  change 5, 14, 20–1, 25–6, 49, 59, 77, 125, 166
  cohesion 13, 20, 165
  justice 24, 47, 94, 124, 127, 136, 170
  movement(s) 5, 47, 99, 165
Stephan, Walter G. 118, 124, 126
Stock, Cheryl 96
Strachan, Jane 6
Suliman, Samid 93
Swick, Kevin 118, 120, 144
Sylvester, Christine 46

Truscott, Stephen D. 118, 120

UN Security Council resolutions 13, 48
United States (US) 2, 4, 7–8, 26, 35–7, 44, 52, 54–9, 75, 86, 91–2, 99–101, 103, 117, 121, 145, 153

violence 2–3, 7, 10–11, 13–14, 20–1, 23–5, 29, 31–7, 46–7, 49–57, 59, 61, 66, 85–7, 89, 92, 105, 112, 115–17, 120–1, 148, 150–3, 155–6, 167, 169
  nonviolence 26, 100, 117

war 4, 12, 20, 29, 30, 35, 44–5, 47, 56
  Cold War 26
  War on Terror 82
Washington DC 7, 9, 12, 28, 36, 151
Wilcox, Lauren B. 3, 23, 155

youth 11, 13–14, 29–30, 37, 45–6, 48–51, 53–4, 57, 60–2, 65–68, 70, 76, 84–7, 93, 97, 99, 120–1, 166, 168–9
  age 9–11, 35, 37, 44–9, 51–4, 58, 61, 67, 87–8, 165
  as programme facilitators 2, 37, 44, 48, 65
  young people 2, 4, 7–10, 33, 35–6, 88–90, 98, 104–5, 123, 145, 160, 170–1
Youth, Peace and Security 13, 45–8

EU authorised representative for GPSR:
Easy Access System Europe, Mustamäe tee 50,
10621 Tallinn, Estonia
gpsr.requests@easproject.com

www.ingramcontent.com/pod-product-compliance
Lightning Source LLC
Chambersburg PA
CBHW071204240426
43668CB00032B/2087